M000223608

Here's what everyday geniuses (just like you) have to say . . .

"I used to think those who are living their dream lives and running their dream businesses are cut from a different cloth, and that I'll never be able to have all of that, but Kelly proved me wrong on all fronts. Kelly has been my #1 role model showing me how to create a life of authenticity and freedom, and making money doing so!"

—Dominique Huang, Program Manager at Microsoft

"Kelly feels like your best-friend-life-coach-hairstylist-guardian-angel all in one!"

—Dr. Jamie Wong, Doctor of Physical Therapy

"Kelly's knowledge on mindset and business is just insane. Listening to her always lights me up, makes me check-in and see things from a new perspective. It's like taking a shot of enthusiasm and motivation."

—Ange Severo, Life Coach + Yoga Teacher

"The content and energy that Kelly brings are absolutely magical. Everything is real, raw, and honest. She's seriously like the big sister I wish I had and aspire to be: unconditionally caring, optimistic, and believes in others. If you want to get some of that energy, listen to her. It will shift your life."

—Julianne Nieh, Entrepreneur

"Before working with Kelly, I had a lingering belief that it wasn't possible for me to help others in an impactful way and make money doing it. Kelly feels like your greatest cheerleader and now building a digital business, making money, and having fun in the process are all doable!"

—Nishi Singhal, Intuition Coach

"Kelly has an innate gift for not only seeing the potential in others but turning that potential into reality. Without Kelly, I truly don't believe I'd be living my dream of running a business and doing work I love that's aligned with my genius."

—Kristy Vail, Life Coach + Writer

P.S. you're a genius

P.S. you're a genius

An unconventional guide to finding your innate gifts (*even when you feel like you have none*)

Kelly Trach

Matt Holt Books
An Imprint of BenBella Books, Inc.
Dallas, TX

BenBella Books, Inc.
10440 N. Central Expressway
Suite 800
Dallas, TX 75231
benbellabooks.com
Send feedback to feedback@benbellabooks.com

BenBella is a federally registered trademark.
Matt Holt and logo are trademarks of BenBella Books.

Printed in the United States of America
10 9 8 7 6 5 4 3 2 1

Library of Congress Control Number: 2021941517
ISBN 9781953295705
eISBN 9781637740040

Editing by Katie Dickman
Copyediting by Jennifer Brett Greenstein
Proofreading by Michael Fedison and Greg Teague
Text design and composition by PerfecType, Nashville, TN
Cover design by Brigid Pearson
Cover image © Shutterstock / Avene
Printed by Lake Book Manufacturing

**Special discounts for bulk sales are available.
Please contact bulkorders@benbellabooks.com.**

To you.
If you've ever felt uncool, not special enough, unlovable,
or perhaps not worthy or deserving, I hope you discover
the opposite through the pages of this book.

CONTENTS

INTRODUCTION

We were all sitting in a circle. The dude leading this weekend program for college students striving to score high-paying jobs after graduation wanted us to introduce ourselves with our name and one fun fact about us. Now, this wasn't just any fact. He specifically said, "Recruiters are looking to see that you won a chess championship in China *and* that you are getting straight As. It's got to be something really memorable and unique about you."

In the jet-black Armani suit that he probably wore to his fancy finance internship in New York, the kid beside me said, "I'm Tom. I'm currently learning ancient Egyptian and becoming fluent in hieroglyphics."

Fuck.

Growing up, I didn't think I was particularly special, and things like this always stumped me.

But it was my turn to go next.

"Hi, I'm Kelly," I gulped.

"I like . . . *mustard.*"

Oh god. Did that just come out of my mouth?

"I, umm, love mustard so much. I will put double the amount of mustard on my burger compared to ketchup. But a veggie burger, because I don't eat meat. You know those Kirkland ones you get at Costco? Yeah, those. So, uh, I guess that's what makes me special. I love mustard. Any kind, actually. Grainy is good. Although honey mustard might be the best."

I could feel the guy at the front of the room rolling his eyes and thinking this extracurricular experience was totally wasted on me. Needless to say, this six-month program didn't work out well for me. The leader hooked up teacher's pets like Tom with connections at Fortune 500 companies while I was told something to the tune of "you're not what these employers are looking for."

I felt like my deepest fear was confirmed: unlike everyone around me, I was not special.

I never thought I was gifted or talented or smart. I just worked hard to get where I was. I graduated high school with a 96 percent average, which was pretty good considering I was in five AP classes. My strategy was to just spend time doing my homework and practice whatever math problem was in front of me. It wasn't a hard equation to crack: do the homework, get good grades, and then people will make a big fuss about how smart you are . . . *which will make up for the fact that you think you're dumb.*

I didn't know what I was really good at. I genuinely believed that there was nothing extraordinarily awesome about me. So I was forever on a quest to figure it out. That way, I could participate in stupid icebreakers and sound semi-decent in a room full of strangers.

I've done all the personality tests. I'm an ENFJ, but all that really told me was that I'm your stereotypical extrovert and I was supposed to be popular like the high school cheerleader or quarterback. (I dunno where that trait was in my teenage years.)

A paid assessment said that "enjoying achievement" was my top strength. (Like, what am I going to do with that? Push myself more and die early of burnout?) My Enneagram says I'm an 8w7. It told me that I was determined, independent, and a nonconformist. And if not channeled correctly, this type tends to be the high school bully. (Well, that's conflicting. I thought I was supposed to be popular?)

I even turned to astrology for answers. I'm a Leo and cheesy internet astrologers with bad websites that haven't been updated since the '90s say that this means I'm highly confident and gregarious, and I love luxury. (How does my love for high-end hotels turn into a career, exactly? I mean, I'd rather vacation there than work for one.)

Whenever you take these tests, or look anywhere outside yourself for answers, you end up with a mixed bag and nothing really accurate. You read the results and think, *Oh! Yes! That's me. Ohhh . . . That's not me. Uh, not that either. Um, I'm sort of like that?* And then you close your Chrome tab.

If you are an overachiever like me, then perhaps you also feel like deep down inside you are a total piece of shit. That your success isn't real because you merely worked hard for it. Or perhaps you are decent at many things and thus have zero significant talents. Or you are a loser like me who doesn't have a jaw-dropping hobby like learning hieroglyphics because you were busy trying to just get by in life.

Whatever story your inner critic has told you about how you are nowhere close to unique, I get it.

Here are some words I previously used to describe myself:

- Stupid. *Everyone else here is way smarter than me.*
- Fraud. *How did I get here? Was this a fluke?*
- Uncool. *I definitely don't belong at the popular table.*
- Average. *My hobbies include music, food, and travel . . . just like everyone else's.*
- Uninteresting. *My work is pretty much my life.*
- Behind. *Everyone else is way farther along than me.*

- Dumb. *Eyebrows get raised when I suggest my ideas, so I'll shut up.*
- Unworthy. *Sure, he can go for that opportunity because he's genuinely bright. I'm nowhere near as good as him.*
- Low-brow. *You need more refined interests.* The Bachelor *doesn't cut it.*
- Weird. *People aren't laughing at your jokes.*
- Straight-up subpar. *You could be so much better at everything in life. From meal prep to having a better budgeting system, everybody is just doing it way better than you.*

Because I felt this way about myself, I found that working hard, well, worked for me. It was my saving grace. If I could get gold stars, then these bad qualities would magically vanish when a teacher circled an A+ at the top of my page in red Sharpie.

If someone said "Great job!" or I got the highest mark in the class, I felt validated. I felt good. I felt like I was making up for my aforementioned negative traits.

Working hard was my strategy to get by. But it all came crashing down about three years after my mustard moment.

Let's fast-forward to my rock bottom. Or, as Brené Brown would say, "spiritual awakening."

It was 2016. It was the wee hours of the early morning and I was in a cedar log cabin in the middle of nowhere. The Wi-Fi and cell reception were bad, so my only option was to "be still with myself" as your annoying one-with-the-universe yoga teacher would say. I needed to stop running away from my problems and address all the crap I'd been sweeping under the rug.

Things were not working. My third start-up was starting to show signs of imminent death and given that my previous two business endeavors had also sunk like the *Titanic*, I needed to get it together.

A major reason for this trip was to help me figure out what I would do with my life. The space away from San Francisco was supposed to help me clear my mind. So I poured myself a coffee and sat down to ponder my options. *Should I look for a job? Find an early-stage start-up to join? Think of another idea and pitch it to Y Combinator? Network my tush off to drum up some opportunities?* I kicked back and stared out the window.

Then I heard it.

What if you just did what you're good at?

It was one of those times when you hear a voice telling you what you should do. And it's not someone else's voice, but your own. Like your smarter, wiser, inner self. Call it God, the source, the universe, or whatever you want. It feels like a cosmic intervention when the shit gets real in your life. It was almost like the big guy upstairs rang my cell and said, "Girl, what in the Lord's name are you doing?"

Like the annoying friend who calls your phone a second time after you sent them to voicemail, the voice rang in my ears again.

What if you just did what you were good at?

This was a question I had never considered. My whole life I did *not* just "do what I was good at."

That would be unimpressive. And pathetic. Back then, I was the hardest hustler you ever met. I got all my validation from struggling and striving to "prove" myself (I'm not exactly sure to whom) and "earn" it (for some unforsaken reason).

Looking back, I see that this pattern started in elementary school when I needed to pass a sixth-grade science test. I wasn't particularly gifted at science, so I had to roll up my sleeves and study. I studied at the kitchen table. I studied on the way to swimming lessons. I even took my flash cards to gym class and reviewed them while I waited for my turn at kickball.

When I got my test back, I saw my score written in red pen at the top of the page.

100 percent.

I was so relieved that I cried.

The strategy of working hard paid off and I kept it up for the rest of the school year. Teachers started loving me and my peers suddenly respected me. Now, I was the "smart kid," which was better than being the random wallflower. You see, I was a dorky kid and my mom gave me bowl cuts at home growing up. Plus, my best friend was my cousin who went to another school. So this recognition was sweet.

I stuck to this strategy through high school and university. I attended one of Canada's most competitive business schools and won a bucket-load of scholarships. Extracurriculars, internships every summer at reputable companies (the ones whose logos you know), and weekend classes were the norm, all accompanied by my dean's-list status, of course. I did competitions in Australia, studied abroad in Paris, and even worked at Tesla Motors selling cars. I was your classic overachiever, go-getter, cram-everything-into-my-calendar-er.

I was wiped. But I was rewarded.

I had two job offers before I graduated. I picked one, signed the papers, and set my start date for September 1. But it was January and I had eight months of spare time on my hands. So I did what every other twenty-one-year-old girl does: I started my first tech start-up.

I quickly fell in love with the challenge and thrill of building something badass, so I emailed that company to tell 'em I couldn't do it anymore. And because Canada isn't exactly the mecca of tech, I moved to San Francisco.

The same habits continued. I worked on my start-up from dawn to dusk. I went to an event every night and networked my ass off. I would show up solo, slap on a name tag, and introduce myself. I went to events at Stanford and rubbed shoulders with important peeps. I had meetings with venture capitalists and investors, angels and advisers. Then I won a full scholarship to study at a pre-accelerator program taught by a billionaire venture capitalist in Silicon Valley. Plus, I picked up extra volunteer work to support a team that was trying to win a $100 million grant with Singularity University's XPRIZE and became buddies with a particular investor for whom I did research on the side.

But my first tech start-up wasn't taking off.

In fact, it was failing.

So I pushed harder. Did more research. Met with more people.

I tried hiring. I emailed every single undergrad in the Stanford computer science program asking them if they wanted an internship.

I tried pivoting. I changed my idea, went after a new market, and tweaked the product offering.

I tried finding a cofounder. I took Uber rides to random dive bars in the Bay Area where they had plastic flamingos, fake grass, and bad music to meet these people.

I tried starting over. After two start-ups failed, I began a third one.

Still, nothing was working. The thing that pissed me off the most was that my usual tactic of "trying harder" wasn't getting me anywhere. This habit had worked for me over the last ten years. So, how could it *not* be holding up now?

It all became oh-so-clear in that cabin when the little voice inside me wouldn't quiet down.

What if you just did what you were good at?

To be honest, I didn't really know *what* I was good at. I was competent at many things (except for sports that involved balls). When I thought of Malcolm Gladwell's ten thousand hours concept, the only thing that came to mind was how I managed my celiac disease and IBS. So I thought I'd be able to share my tips 'n' tricks with some other gal out there on the internet who'd also puff up like a balloon when she ate a whole wheat bagel. So, in response to that question from my inner voice, I had the idea that maybe I could try an online business instead. Like a blog or something centered on this whole "healthy living" thing.

Maybe it's because I'm an entitled millennial or I secretly believe my ideas are better than everyone else's, but I knew I couldn't go back to working for someone else. So if I was going to be smart enough (or dumb enough, depending on how you slice it) to build another business, I had to do things differently.

I had some rules for myself since I had a track record of entrepreneurial embarrassments. It had to be easy. It had to be cheap. (No investors. My budget was $5,000 in expenses for the whole year.) It had to be 100 percent digital (cuz that's the cheapest). I had to use what I had on hand. (No new fancy gear.) It had to rely on passive income. (No more hustling for cash.) I had to be able to do everything entirely myself. (Meaning no cofounders who could code.) It had to be grassroots. (No paid advertising.) It had to be simple and practical. (No more moonshot innovations like my idea to supply food to the people on Mars when Elon and his friends move there.) It had to be built around the things that came most naturally to me. And I had one year to try.

It started as a health blog where I talked about my holistic approach to my autoimmune condition, which had a large emphasis on mindset. Half a year in, I discovered that mindset was more my style and dropped the health blogging. I created my first online course, launched my podcast, and started taking life-coaching clients after getting requests for it. People waltzed up to me and asked if I could coach them. At this point, I had a solid online presence, including a great website, a thriving podcast, online courses, e-books, and, most importantly, paying customers. People started asking how I built my business and if I could help them accomplish the same. To be honest, business coaching wasn't on my radar. Yet someone asked if they could hire me. I said YOLO. (Actually, I wrote a very professional email.) The story ends with me quickly realizing I was stupid for trying health blogging and life coaching because business was, and always had been, my jam. I just hadn't seen it.

By scratching my head and wondering, *Gosh, what am I actually good at?* I inadvertently stumbled upon my genius. And long story short, I built a six-figure business.

For the last several years, I've been working as a sought-after business coach who helps people find their genius and monetize it so that they can build digital businesses. In addition, I host *The Kelly Trach Show*, a top-rated podcast with over 100K downloads, and I teach my online courses and curriculum to students all over the world.

The framework that I'm teaching you in this book was something I developed for my coaching clients simply as a way for me to understand them. I'd ask certain questions to find their gifts and, in turn, see how their unique genius could be translated into a business model. As a result, my clients scored customers within forty-eight hours of launching, handed in resignation letters at their nine-to-fives within six weeks, booked speaking gigs at Google within one month of being open for business, and outearned their corporate salaries by the end of their first year.

Now, each client's business was entirely different. Everyone had different niches, personalities, and locations, from Singapore to Australia to London. Yet there was one common denominator to their success: they were doing their genius.

When I mastered my framework with clients, I taught it in my signature course called Your Conscious Empire™. When you're taking things to the masses via an online course, this is the ultimate litmus test: Do they like it? Does this *actually* work for everyone? Can this be taught in a general way and not just during a personal call? Am I, Kelly Trach, actually a genius . . . or a total dumbass? No one knows unless I try.

One of the first modules of that course is called "Find Your Genius and Monetize It," and oodles of students raved about it. It helped them find their purpose, figure out what to sell, stand out in a saturated market, and unearth what made them uniquely qualified to serve others when, in the past, impostor syndrome had stopped them in their tracks. My framework was the catalyst for helping them book $1,000 clients, leave full-time jobs, and find that spark they'd been yearning for. When I heard that consistent feedback, I knew I had something special.

Although my framework was initially built for entrepreneurs, what you'll discover in this book is applicable to everyone. If you are a high school grad, quarter-life-crisis-er, or someone who wants to switch careers, this book is for you. It's for entrepreneurs and soon-to-be ones. College kids, side hustlers, and the folks who've been laid off who are looking for new work. Lastly, it's for the peeps who already have a good career but just want to spend more time doing what they adore.

Now, I want to help you find your genius.

With this book, you'll discover your top three to five gifts through self-reflective exercises. (Short homework. I promise.) Then, we'll combine those gifts to find your genius. I'll show you where you're already doing it so that you can witness it in your current life and illuminate new ways to express it so that you can do more meaningful work *more often*.

Next, you'll ditch the doubts that hold you back from sharing your genius with the world. (Doubts I had myself.) Ones like *I can't make money doing that* and *someone's already doing it better than me, so I can't*. And the good 'ol *I'm not good enough*.

Once you realize that you're a genius, you'll need a better playbook. I'll teach you some new-school rules for success. You'll discover lessons like "throw out everything you know and go with how it feels" and "nobody can do it just like you, no matter how hard they try." These are the lessons I've learned from my winding journey with more downs than ups.

So, what does this all mean for you?

Finding your genius is about courageously listening to the hollerings of your heart, perhaps for the first time in your life, in the most vulnerable moments when it feels like everything's at stake. It's about witnessing your own value and innately knowing that you have an undeniable brilliance—even if no one believes in you (and you doubt yourself). Most importantly, it's about finding your self-worth and knowing how to put your skills to use and convincingly convey your value to anyone.

When you know your genius, you instinctively understand the work you should be doing in the world, what makes you oh-so-special (even if you don't feel special at all), and how to position yourself when you're interviewing for jobs or starting a new business. Ultimately, it's about honoring your gifts so deeply that you create an outcome that is truly world-class and makes you indispensable.

So, what if you could discover that you have timeless gifts inside you that can always be turned into a career, regardless of economic trends? Arguably, the work you were born to do? Where nobody can replace you and no robot can mimic your intellect and heart through an algorithm? What if you could be the vessel of deep service to the world that you crave? And get paid properly to do it? What if your genius gave you the license to unlock the full certainty and complete courage to go after what you've always wanted? The strategy on how you crack open your brilliance comes packed inside the pages of this book.

So here's how to find yours . . .

chapter 1

The Definition of Genius

Lemme answer the million-dollar question 'round here. (Okay, not million dollar. You paid, like, twenty bucks for this book, so let me answer the twenty-dollar question.)

What the heck is your genius?

The dictionary has its own definition, but this is how I distinctly define it: **Your genius is the combination of your top three to five gifts working together to create world-class expertise doing something only you can do.**

You can call it "being in the zone" or your "je ne sais quoi" or your "it factor." Maybe you know those "superstars" in your office who just can do no wrong and somehow always get the promotion. Some people just have that "magic touch" (which sounds like the name of a sex shop, but I digress). Others have the "special sauce" or "secret ingredient" or "X factor." It's that thing that's so hard to define, yet everyone talks about and really friggin' wants.

It's when you look at people who are so dang good at what they do and think, *How can I get a piece of that?* Steve Jobs had it in spades. Elon Musk just puts everyone else to shame. And Steven Spielberg was doing it way before it was cool. Think about the way Aretha Franklin belts out "R-E-S-P-E-C-T" and makes you wanna take singing classes immediately. Or how Jerry Seinfeld makes hosting a TV show and getting coffee with comedians in classic cars look like the best thing in the world. All those things are displays of "genius." And yours is not as elusive as you think.

My framework is simple. You unlock your genius when you take your top three to five gifts, weave 'em together, and perform a task that involves all of them. You know you're rooted in your genius when it comes ridiculously natural to you, feels fun to fabricate, and you craft an expert-level final product that others would struggle to produce.

Now, you're probably wondering, *Okay, Kelly, how is this different from finding my strengths?* It's different in several key ways.

1. There's a difference between being "strong" and being "gifted."

Your genius is built upon your gifts. "Strong" indicates that there is room for improvement, but "gifted" implies something innate. You can be good at many things, which is why I separate a strength from a gift. Personally, I define a strength as a talent that you can perform better than others. Strengths are generally good qualities, but they can keep you stuck doing work that's "above average." You'll be solid but not exceptional.

Yet some of your strengths are top-tier. These are your gifts. *Gift* is a far better word since you are truly gifted at these activities. Plus, you don't have to "try" to be good at them—you naturally are. In my framework, we separate strengths from gifts so that we know what to focus on.

2. Your genius already exists.

You don't need to develop it more or proverbially sharpen the saw. (Radical, I know.) You could do it right now on the spot for me and even Simon Cowell would give you a score of 10.

3. Your genius is a synergistic expression.

While *synergy* sounds like an overused word you'd read in some stuffy corporate company's mission statement, this synergistic combination of your gifts makes the outcome stronger than the sum of the parts.

Unlike the traditional notion of strengths, this framework isn't just about one trait working overtime for you. You can't just rely on one thing and call yourself a genius. ("Guys, I'm great at communicating! I'm a genius! Time to crack open a beer and call it a day!") Your genius surfaces when you harness all your top gifts at once. Let me elaborate with a cheesy metaphor.

There is an old tale about two oxen. One ox by itself can carry one ton of weight. Yet if you have two oxen, they can carry three tons together.

Is this scientifically correct? I don't know. Is this a good metaphor? Yes. Your genius is a lot like this because when you perform a project that harnesses all three to five gifts at once, you get an exponentially large payoff.

4. You can't find your genius from a list.

Most folks discover their best qualities from looking at a list of common traits and seeing what resonates with them, yet your genius is as personal as your fingerprint. It can't be found in a boring book or in an index of strengths that you Googled before you rewrote your résumé. It's soul-level work that needs to be done by you. Plus, quizzes and assessments can take you only so far. Usually, they take into account only a few dozen qualities. But what about the countless other gifts out there? The weird ones? The quirky ones? And what about the gifts that can only be felt by the human heart? Like singing or dancing? Or painting or writing? Code and algorithms can't pick up on that.

5. It shows you where to focus your energy.

For many years, I was passionately driven, but I didn't know what to pursue. It was like I had a car with a full tank of gas, but I didn't know where to drive it. So I was wasting my energy doing doughnuts in the parking lot. That's an issue with strengths: you can have a lotta 'em and they can keep you going in circles. For example, when I'd have an intuitive hit about something that turned out to be true, I'd be like, *Sooo . . . am I a psychic now?* Or when I got praise at my job leading birthday parties, I was like, *Is cutting ice cream cake my calling?* When we look solely at our genius, the destination becomes obvious.

6. It's simple.

I am biased, but I find other strategies to be vague and overwhelming. Which is not good when you are in the middle of a dear-sweet-Jesus-what-should-I-do-with-my-life crisis and need answers delivered as fast as Amazon Prime Now's one-hour delivery. (None of that five-to-seven business days shit.)

I once took an assessment for about one hundred bucks to discover my strong suits. It gave me a list of forty-nine things that I was good at. *Forty-nine?!* What the hell am I supposed to do with all of that? Too much information that features charts, icons, and other crap is confusing. It took me about an hour to understand the color-coded legend itself. Of course, you're going to be good at many things. But it's almost impossible to brainstorm a career when you're taking forty-nine traits into account at once. Focusing on your top three to five is far more actionable.

Now, how did I discover this?

I stumbled on my genius by accident. Like when you're bumbling around for salty munchies in the cupboard after too many Mary-J-infused peach gummies and find an old bag of salt 'n' vinegar chips in the back.

I realized that as I built my fourth business, I was weirdly harnessing all my best gifts and abilities. When I yanked back the layers to see what made this one successful, I understood that my success came from tapping into my genius. Plus, I only found it when I dumped all the crap that looked good on paper, waved my white flag, and worked on the stuff that felt good to create.

Things started to click. For starters, building this business was easy (I had already built three before and attended business school) and I practiced my ninja-level marketing skills (which is what I majored in). I was in my element and creating constantly. I loved developing new products, writing sales pages, and brainstorming new ways to spread the word.

Plus, I was also teaching a ton. I would teach topics in my weekly podcast and coach clients for hours on end. I was making e-books, courses, and programs. I was stellar at breaking things down step-by-step and making it easy for people to implement.

Then, it came to speaking. Between creating podcast episodes and recording loads of videos for my online classes, I became an even better speaker. I was always talking (which I loved, anyway) and I didn't even mind peeing every hour on the hour from all the water I was drinking when my throat became dry.

Now, there were certain tasks that made me feel like I was "doing the work I was born to do" and "living my purpose" and all those other barf-bag cheesy phrases that business books like to use. These tasks were ridiculously simple for me, were always fun, and yet serendipitously yielded the highest results in my business.

1. Coaching clients
2. Podcasting
3. Creating online courses
4. Hosting webinars

They always had four gifts in common: teaching, speaking, creating, and connecting.

Although I was strong at all four gifts individually, when I pursued projects that aligned them all, I felt like a firecracker. I was in the flow, I loved it, and I was making money. This was a big deal given that my previous businesses paid me diddly-squat.

I realized I'd hit some sort of jackpot.

Looking back, this fourth business was accidentally built on my genius. Podcasting was my main marketing channel (teaching content was a piece of cake), webinars were my sales mechanism (anything cheaper than selling a $100,000 Tesla felt stupidly simple), and I made money from selling my coaching packages and online courses (two activities I loved doing). I kinda kept thinking, *Jeez, I can't believe they pay me for this.*

Look, all I did was find my genius and focus on it. Which pretty much makes me look really brilliant despite the fact that I had a bowl cut for years and failed calculus twice.

For a long time, I definitely did *not* think I was a genius. I thought, *Don't you need to be, like, super smart or something? Or join Mensa? Or be invited to work at the Pentagon?*

But being a "genius" is not reserved for folks with Ivy League degrees or brainiacs who sold their software companies at eighteen. The word *genius* is actually reserved for you if you have the courage to claim your gifts.

Everybody has a form of remarkable genius inside them. (Yes, even you. No matter how pathetic you think you are.)

It's just a matter of finding it.

chapter 2

Why Finding Your Genius Creates the Success You've Always Desired

There are ten key reasons why finding your genius is a game changer.

1. You'll be seen as a thought leader and the go-to expert in your field.

When you're doing the thing you were born to do, people notice and heads turn. You can attract more established clients or work with cooler companies that have missions that align with your heart. Dream projects, TV appearances, and invites to be a guest on your favorite podcasts might flow your way. Plus, people consider you a "guru" and seek your advice. These things are all possible when you build a living based on your genius.

Let's look at one of my clients, Kristy. Years ago, she was an interior designer and hired me to help her start her own design business. To attract clients and build her community, she launched a podcast that embodied her approach to design: it was about feeling aligned in all areas of your life, not just your space. She shared with her listeners how to create intentional living in your home, in your relationships, and with yourself. One day she asked me what she should really be doing with her life, based on how much she loved connecting with like-hearted podcast guests and interviewing them. I said, "I know this is out of left field, but I think it's life coaching." From knowing Kristy well, I could spot her genius. She was great at truly hearing people and seeing them. I knew she had a knack for listening, supporting, and asking the deeper questions that would transform not just people's spaces but their lives. I also noticed that her podcast listeners and design clients had personalities similar to hers. They were sensitive, creative women. Plus, they were asking her more about life than interior design. I told her to give coaching a try. She booked her first paid client within forty-eight hours of launching her coaching packages. Now, she's a life coach for creative, sensitive, and introverted women and helps them show up more confidently in the world. Kristy is now the go-to gal in that niche and outearns her corporate salary doing this, sometimes making up to triple what she used to earn on a monthly basis.

2. You'll cash in on your greatest gifts and what comes most naturally to you.

This is where it gets really good: your gifts are already top-tier traits of yours—you love doing them, and all you have to do is keep focusing on where it feels fun.

My client Di worked at Sony's Sydney, Australia, office for fourteen years as a senior marketing manager. But at the boardroom table she would daydream about her workouts and what kind of fitness routine she'd do after the clock hit five. (She's the kind of gal who loves burpees, so you know that fitness is really her forte.) One day, she decided to get qualified to follow her fitness passion and start her own fitness classes. She coupled her love for fitness with her own journey: helping mamas return to fitness after baby. Di noticed that there were few fitness options for new mothers that accommodated their babies, so her in-person group sessions offered a complimentary sideline nanny service that made it a no-brainer for clients. Plus, her approach was different. She noticed after the birth of her son that there was such high pressure for women to "bounce back" after baby and "do it all." Instead, Di believes that postnatal fitness should be a gradual process with more education about recovery and the need for a strong support network of like-minded mamas. Instead of concentrating on "instant abs" and how fast you could fit into your jeans, Di's sessions were focused on creating energy and strength, while reducing the stress of family life. Fast-forward years later, and today Di runs a business that's done half a million in sales. She simply cashed in on what came most naturally to her, and now it's her job to keep teaching fitness and doing what she loves.

3. You'll earn what you're really worth.

When you've honed in on what makes you an expert, you can feel confident asking for that raise or seeking out a higher salary, and in an entrepreneurial setting you can pretty much charge whatever you want. Because when you're great at what you do and everyone else knows it, you'll literally look at your bank account and think, *Holy crap!* Chances are your current work might not be 100 percent tailored to your truest genius. But once you step into it, your income can go *wayyy* up.

Let's do the math here. My first job offer after business school was for $60,000 per year, for a 40-hour workweek. Meaning, 2,080 hours per year at a desk. Instead, with my business, I could book nine clients at my $7,000 coaching package and it would take me only 324 hours to coach them all.

So, do you wanna spend 2,080 hours to make $60,000? Or 342 hours to make $63,000? That's the difference between a year and only 42 workdays. That's the power of finding your genius.

4. You'll tap into total flow and work will feel almost effortless.

As a society, we've been conditioned to work really hard and believe that we can only make money if we grind it out. That's not how I look at it. Because you'll be doing what comes most effortlessly to you, work won't really feel like "work." Instead, it will feel like play. So think about what you adore doing most in life and imagine *that* filling up your time from nine to five. Sounds pretty good, right? That's called being in "the flow," when time disappears and you feel like you could do it forever. It's the kind of work that energizes you and brings you joy, and you never get tired of it. Instead of always waiting for your lunch break, you're so lost in your work that you're like, *What? It's lunch already?* Quite often we feel this stopping of time when we're working on hobbies, spending fun afternoons with friends, or taking vacations. But this is how you can feel in your day job or side hustle as well.

My client Lauren hired me as her business coach because she wanted to start monetizing her fashion blog. At the time, she was a full-time dentist and had been blogging for six years on the side. Lauren loves simple yet elegant style and capsule wardrobes. Her true genius was creating content for her followers. When Lauren pairs outfits together, photographs her flat lays, and showcases different ways to style outfits in a capsule wardrobe, she finds flow. She could talk about style for hours. She knows everything about minimal fashion and maximizing the utility of your wardrobe. While many people find it hard to look effortlessly pulled together, this is really easy for Lauren. And, lo and behold, this is her genius. Since then, Lauren has started collaborating with aligned brands that pay her to create content to promote their products through styling, photography, and blog writing. The result? Lauren has maintained her dentistry career and turned her passion project into a side hustle.

5. You'll attract opportunities versus always promoting yourself.

People will flock to you since you're the best at what you do. When you're in your genius, you've mastered the art of attraction versus promotion because people come to you. Plus, when people know that you're the pro, it annihilates any desire to pick your competitor's product or choose the other gal who's up for the promotion. You'll be like a magnet for people who want to work with you, hire you, or buy your stuff. This all-star status comes from actively proclaiming your gifts and not being shy about them. And, in turn, the seas will part for you.

For example, look at my client Regena. She was a product manager for twelve years at a major tech company. She was getting paid $250,000 per year, but was unfulfilled and felt unvalued by the engineers she managed. One day, a male engineer explosively questioned her leadership and yelled, "Don't you tell me what my team does!" (Even though she led the team.) She was taken aback and wondered, *Was it because I don't have a computer science background, or because I'm a woman of color, or maybe because of how I said it?* That was the final straw. Regena quit. She came to me because she wanted to be a mindfulness teacher instead and coach other women in tech who felt burned out, unseen, and unheard. She already had her mindfulness teaching certification and oodles of experience mentoring junior employees and loved supporting rising female talent. Within one month of launching her business, Google reached out and asked if she could do a paid talk at their headquarters. Once you step into the work you were born to do, the cosmos conspires and cool shit happens.

6. You'll score more prestigious clients or dream job opportunities.

One of my best friends has recruiters knocking on her door 24/7. "Oh! That's Facebook calling again. Yeah, I'm not interested." Another pal got accepted to the Harvard MBA program, the Stanford MBA program, and Y Combinator and was offered a promotion all in one year. One gal I know is a life coach for royal families. Have you ever scratched your head and wondered, *Man, how the heck do people get these good fortunes?* Especially if you've been slogging away begrudgingly at something for years and not getting the traction you desire, seeing others get handed golden opportunities on a silver platter just seems preposterous. When people know that you are the best in your field, they come knocking with projects, requests to be your client, and job opportunities. If you want to start working for some really cool people, then you gotta know this: getting your lucky break is an easy feat if you're doing your genius.

One of my coaching clients, Jena, is a graphic designer. She was working full-time for a company and doing freelance work in the wee hours of the night. Jena hired me because she wanted to work only for herself. We launched her business and right away she scored her first $1,000 client. Within six weeks, she handed in her resignation letter and was working for herself full-time. (Super fast, I know.) The craziest part of all this was the kismet opportunity that came out of the blue. One day, Jena got a message from a well-known podcaster. Jena had been following this person's work for years, had taken her courses, and had listened religiously to her podcast.

This gal had seen the graphics Jena designed and wanted to hire her. First for a small project, and then for her whole dang website. Good fortunes happen to those who do their genius. From celebrity customers to opportunities to work with the best in the biz, I see it all the time with my clients.

7. You'll automatically stand out from the crowd.

Most people are average. That's what the word *average* means, anyway. But how do you become world-class? How do you become the best in your office? Or field? Or country? You do this is by finding your genius and delivering the gifts only you have. In today's economy, there are a multitude of vendors, consultants, or teammates that could be hired for a single job. There are hundreds of people vying for a single position or trying to capture your attention (and credit card) online. So, how do you stand out from the sea of folks doing similar stuff to you? How do you get your résumé to the top of the pile? How do you become the first pick of the team? How do you become indispensable? When you lean into your genius, you master the science of standing out.

8. You'll see your own value.

By knowing your genius, you'll increase your self-worth. You'll be seeing this term a lot, so I want you to understand what I mean by it: self-worth is how highly you regard yourself and the standards you're willing to accept. (This comes in all forms, BTW. From how much you settle in shitty relationships because you don't think you can do better to avoiding asking for what you deserve when the barista gets your coffee order wrong. But for now, we're going to focus on work.)

High self-worth means you value yourself and your gifts. You know what you'll take as a paycheck versus pass on. Plus, you're a pro at saying no and walking away when it's not right. You respect yourself and think you're awesome (in a good, non-conceited way, of course). It's negotiating, asking for what you want, and being up front about it. And not taking any shit either.

Low self-worth is not valuing your genius, not even knowing what it is, and thus settling due to a lack mindset and fear. It's playing small, not seeing your gifts, and not living into the full truth of who you really are. It looks like shying away, dimming down your light, and settling for scraps. It's living a life of "have tos" versus "want tos" because you never really believed in yourself enough to go for it.

One of the quickest ways to get into your worth is by waking up to how freaking awesome you are. Because when you realize how strong and powerful your innate genius is, you'll automatically feel more confident in your abilities. (Which is way better than beating the drum of the old story that you suck, you're a tool, and Wendy from work is way better than you'll ever be.) Finding your genius gives you the license to go after what you want and the confidence to claim it.

9. You'll get where you've always wanted to go.

Small changes now lead to big differences down the road because every moment defines your destiny. When two airplanes depart from LAX, the difference between landing in London versus New York in a handful of hours is only a few degrees at the start. Because if two planes point their noses in slightly different directions at takeoff, even though it's barely noticeable, the final destination after time in flight is significantly different. What's incremental amounts to the extraordinary. So finding your genius *now* gives you a huge leg up down the road. Because nothing is worse than spending all that time and money on a trip to London only to find yourself still an ocean away. Most people wrongly assume that their present-moment actions don't matter. They think there's still "lots of time" to chase dreams or switch careers. The problem is that they don't forecast the long-term impact of staying in misaligned roles or settling for work that's incongruent with their genius. Because, like the trajectory of the two airplanes, what you do now affects where you'll wind up in a decade.

Let me tell you about Tera. She recognized early that she had a gift for swimming. When she was seven, she watched the Olympics on TV and said to her parents, "Wow, I want to do that!" That night, Tera taped a picture of the Olympic rings to her bedroom ceiling. That way, she could see them when she woke up and went to bed. Nurturing that gift early enabled her to go to the Olympics in 2012 when she was nineteen. But what if she hadn't spotted it? What if she'd let her fears get in the way? Your destiny is defined by the decisions you make now. For Tera, it was the difference between aiming for a spot on the podium and still doin' laps at the local pool. The same goes for you: finding your genius is the difference between where you wanna go and where you're stuck right now.

10. You'll find what you've been looking for.

Being rooted in your genius is incredible. And a lot of cool things can happen. But unlike so many other authors of books on success, I'm not going to tell you that it's automatic or guaranteed. I can't promise that you'll make boatloads of money. And I can't promise that you'll become Instagram famous. What I can promise you is that you'll feel awesome, feel good enough, and feel like you've finally "found it." You'll have days when you love what you do so much that it can make you cry. You'll no longer lie in bed on Sunday nights resenting the workweek ahead or worry that you're on the wrong career trajectory.

These stories that I've shared with you are of people who did the work, put their heart out there, and showed up courageously in their genius. Even when they heard no, got rejected, and doubted the whole damn thing. My hope is that you keep going. All I can say is this: your genius is worth it. The fulfillment that your soul craves is sitting on the other side of fear. Your most authentic life is on the other side of doubt. And access to your true life's purpose is on the flip side of failure. I can't guarantee that you'll ever see a dime or you'll become the next Zuckerberg, but I *can* guarantee that you'll find the feeling that you've been missing.

Part 1

How to Find Your Gifts

In this section of the book, I'm going to ask you ten questions to help you find your innate gifts. Your job is to keep a running list of everything that comes up. It's okay if there's overlap. For now, write it all down.

chapter 3

How Do Your Idols Illuminate Your Gifts?

I have a mild (okay, full-blown) obsession with Jen Sincero. You know, the one who wrote *You Are a Badass*. It started with reading that book and snowballed into devouring her every interview and listening to her audiobooks so many times that I recited lines like a parrot. Every day, I'd crack open one of Jen's books to a random page and treat it like a tarot card deck to see what she had to say to me (personally). My Jen Sincero frenzy reached its peak in 2018 when I met her and she signed my highly cherished copy of *You Are a Badass at Making Money* with the sentiment "Kelly, here's to getting fabulously rich."

I respect Jen Sincero's work immensely. There's something about her that has drawn me in like a magnet. Because I'm the creep that I am, I even noticed in one of her book headshots that her gold necklace says "Leo" on it, which made my heart do a backflip since I'm a Leo too. I think Jen is wildly hilarious and super authentic; she's a tells-it-like-it-is kinda gal who has the gumption to play big and see what she can get away with. Jen goes for what she wants in life and has the audacity to pull it off without questioning her desires or limiting herself. She's like that cool older sister you've always wanted who will let you have a puff of her cigarette and not tell Mom that you're out late with your boyfriend. (I mean, I've met the chick for, like, five minutes at a book signing, but this is what I've garnered from her books.) Jen knows her worth, charges what she wants unapologetically, and has made a living off of being her genuine self.

Ready for me to blow your mind?

What you admire in others is a direct reflection of your own genius.

The qualities you treasure in your idols are actually the talents inside you. Identifying those qualities is the fastest way to find your own gifts.

Chances are, there are a few people who you've admired for years now. Maybe you've followed their career trajectories, been longtime fans of theirs, or looked up to them because they were a few years ahead of you in school. The greatness you see in them is the greatness you have inside you.

Everything that I listed about Jen is actually a reflection of me and what I'm really great at. How comforting is it to know that the people you praise are simply reflecting back a source of untapped potential inside you? And even on your darkest days, when you feel like the sun will never shine again, just remember that you hold that unwavering magic too. No matter how much you fumbled in the meeting, or how often you said the wrong thing, or how much your ex broke your heart, it's there and will never fade. Sometimes, that's just the hope I need to keep going.

Can I tell you an honest story? Getting this book published wasn't exactly a slice of cake. The book business is like the acting industry: you need an agent to represent you. A lot of literary agents thought that my theory was weird, that I didn't have enough followers, or that it should be a totally different book. ("Can you please write about workplace negotiation?" "Uh, no?") When I felt fed up, my eyes wandered to my bookshelf and I'd see the works of Brené Brown, Jen Sincero, and Gabby Bernstein sitting there. It was easy to think, *Maybe they're right. Who the hell will ever listen to what I have to say?* You have to remember that somewhere, somehow—and even though you might not feel like it today—**your admiration for your idols reflects your own capacity to do the same**.

On a particularly rough day pitching this book to agents, I Googled "Jen Sincero quotes" to seek some inspiration. (Because after two hundred rejection letters, it's pretty easy to feel like your writing is maybe the most foul rubbish in the history of humankind.) Going down a rabbit hole, I found out that Jen and I have the same birthday. Which made me feel like the cosmos did in fact agree with my theory that what we admire in others is a reflection of our own genius. I took it as a sign to keep going.

So look at the top five people you admire. Take a moment and think about who you've looked up to the longest. Go big here. (And don't pick Sam from the grocery store who bags your carrots nicely every time.) Really dream here. Who do you think is cool? Who do you look up to? Who have you idolized for a long time? Write down five names.

Then, I want you to share five qualities that you absolutely love about each of them. What makes them irresistible to you? Why do you hang on their every word? What traits are so alluring to you? Which qualities do you deeply respect?

Based on what you wrote down, notice which gifts might actually be yours too.

Now, how do we turn this into something that pays the bills?

If you are reading this book because you don't know WTF you should do with your life, then I have a follow-up question for you: How are all these folks who you admire making money?

What are their careers? What are they selling? How are they earning an income? This might take some Googling. Are they speakers, consultants, or managers of membership sites? Are they all VPs at major social enterprises that have a strong ethos of giving back? Are they making money on song royalties or sales commissions? Chances are, they are all earning a living in a similar way. (If not, look for themes. For example, are they all executives in leadership positions? Agents of change? Creative types?) Write this down.

For example, let's look at my business in relation to Jen Sincero's. She offers books (check), courses (definitely, check), and speaking (yup), and formerly did coaching (ditto!).

This exercise provides telling insights into what you should be doing for work because you'll subconsciously gravitate toward your own genius. (It will be like some part of you knew all along.) And when you're done, you might see the desires you've never admitted out loud or always thought were impossible.

As you study how these peeps are monetizing their genius, I want you to look for common themes. This is your map to cashing in on what comes most naturally to you. Believe it or not, you have the capacity to do exactly this with your life. Your truth is your own power. So, when you have the clarity to accept what you've always wanted, you're on the verge of a miracle.

Your turn:

- Write down the five people you admire most. Then write down five things that you like about each of them. (Yup, that's twenty-five traits total. Some traits might repeat.) Ask yourself: Which of these are actually my gifts?
- Write down how all these people are making money. Ask yourself: How could I do this too?

chapter 4

What Are You Great at That Nobody Taught You How to Do?

I recently was talking to this HR lady at a major corporation about leading a workshop at their office. Let's just say she really subscribed to the old-school notions of success. After grilling me about my background and experience, she posed her final question: "Do you have a certified degree to coach clients?" I don't. School of hard knocks, baby. But I found myself trying to prove that I had the background. Trying to convince her. Trying to wow her with my client success stories. It felt like I was on *Shark Tank* or I was pitching myself to Meryl Streep's character in *The Devil Wears Prada*. She concluded with her final, dismal remark: "We are looking for real experts with proper backgrounds."

Ouch. There it was again. My lack of formal training.

When I started coaching clients, I used to get embarrassed whenever someone asked me if I had any "qualifications" to do that. I knew other coaches who went to pricey $20,000 programs to get certified or did their masters in executive leadership coaching at fancy colleges. When I saw that, I thought my life experience and personal interest in the subject didn't count in the same way that their degrees did.

Nobody taught me how to coach; I just kinda knew how to do it. Because I had no proper education on the ins and outs of coaching, I always felt like it was a big, black mark on my résumé when people looked at it. Despite my bachelor's degree in business and my entrepreneurial experience, I never felt like they were enough to actually "coach" someone on the subject.

On the flip side, I had years of experience in part-time teaching jobs. I was gifted at seeing potential in people, asking meaningful questions, identifying patterns, and noticing where people were getting stuck. This skill set stemmed from tutoring, being a teaching assistant, and working as a swim instructor for six years to hundreds of kids with fluttering legs, orange arm floaties, and that slight panic in their eyes as they worried they'd drown. (Don't worry, nobody did.) In university, I gravitated toward roles that let me mentor younger students. Specifically, the coveted position of "orientation week leader" in which you were given a group of twelve incoming wide-eyed and bushy-tailed freshmen to mentor. I took them under my wing, helped them choose their majors, and provided a good listening ear for school struggles and breakups alike.

I had the right skill set to be a coach: loving, yet firm; encouraging, yet pushing you out of your comfort zone; patient, yet holding you to your deadlines; high vibe, yet calling you on your BS. When it came to the business coaching I was doing, my clients wanted to create what I had already done, so I was simply teaching what I knew.

Previous teaching roles + seeing potential + mentorship experience + helping others create the same success I had = slice of cake.

Here's the aha moment I want you to have: **You don't need to go to school for your genius.** One of the worst things you can do is write off the stuff you're innately good at because you didn't formally learn how to do it.

A bad habit people have is assuming that only academic education counts. Don't dismiss your most genuine traits and abilities just because you don't have a plaque on the wall with your name written on it. Four years of school and a piece of paper don't automatically make you special. (They actually can make you a cog in the wheel if you're not careful.)

Self-taught people are some of the best masters. So an easy way to find your gifts is to answer this question: What are you great at that nobody taught you how to do?

Here are three deeper questions to help you figure it out.

1. **Where have you found your own formula?**

   Self-taught folks figured out their own formula. They've taken the recipe and added their own flair. They said, "Screw it, I'm doin' it like this!" Society doesn't always like self-taught folks because they go against "the system" and "how we do it 'round here." But geniuses are rebels and misfits. Questioners and innovators. Makers, movers, and status quo shakers.

   Maybe you've found your own knack or way of doing things that goes against the grain of conventional wisdom. Maybe you've studied something independently because you love it, or picked up a bunch of different pieces and said, "Hey, I think I just made a better puzzle."

   So, what's your formula? What's your way of doing things? Your knack? Your read on the situation? Your innate wisdom that you're adding to the conversation? What's your flow or framework? Your better process or product?

   One of my clients, Nishi, has a bachelor's degree in psychology and spent ten years working in public health. Growing up, Nishi had anxiety. She was a sensitive child and found herself taking on other people's opinions and plans for her life, rather than considering what she wanted. After experiencing career burnout, she sought out talk therapy and self-development, which led her down the path of discovering intuition, getting her yoga teacher training, and graduating from health coaching school. One day, she started wondering, *Wait a second, what feels true for me?* Based on everything she learned, Nishi developed her own knack for combating anxiety through listening to the wisdom within. In her own words, she used "a little bit of everything" she learned along the way. A few years later, she started teaching others how to listen to their intuition too. So, what happened? As Nishi describes it, her "type A, control freak" persona slowly faded away and she got her joy back. What's even better? She left a nine-to-five job, tapped into her creative spirit, and even wrote a book. Nishi now runs her own business and is a stellar example of how finding your own formula can yield great results.

2. **What do you know intuitively?**

What tasks can you automatically do, with little thought, preparation, or effort? For me, I know how to create and make things. It started when I was four and I learned how to braid my own hair. Nobody taught me how to—I simply figured it out myself. In grade school, I fell in love with jewelry. I would buy beads, wire, and just assemble stuff at home with a pair of pliers I found in the house. For my podcast and courses, I never took a class on curriculum design or how to teach things to people—I just knew how to do it. Your intuitive knowledge will always unearth your greatest gifts.

So, what did you figure out on your own? What comes naturally to you? Think of the talents and abilities you have, but never formally learned how to do.

One of my clients, Marina, went to business school and works at a major tech company. She's got a six-figure job that has taken her to New York and San Francisco. Yet one of Marina's true gifts is singing and songwriting. In a coaching session, I asked her, "So, how many years have you been doing this?" She said, "Fifteen." Then I asked, "About how many songs have you written?" And she nonchalantly said, "I dunno, a thousand? At least. I easily write over 150 new songs per year." Holy crap. Nobody taught her how to write songs in the early days—she just did it on her own. Marina's childhood interests naturally gravitated toward music: from playing violin in an orchestra to taking singing and guitar lessons. After fifteen years of songwriting, Marina was accepted into a music production course at Juilliard. She is now taking her gift and writing custom theme songs for film clients in the hours after her nine-to-five ends. She's a perfect example of having a seriously awesome skill set that came naturally and that she refined and mastered over time.

3. **What have you studied independently?**

If you've found your own way to master something by taking interest in a topic and then studying the bejesus outta it from blogs, articles, and workshops, then it totally counts.

What did you learn on your own? What do you study for fun? What topics have you researched so much that you're now fluent in the lingo? What have you always had a natural inclination toward?

One of my clients, Kerri, spent fifteen years in high-paying finance jobs. From a young age, Kerri knew that numbers were just her thing. She was the kind of gal who had a spreadsheet for everything. An aptitude for math led her into a career as a chartered professional accountant and she worked at a Big Four accounting firm in Bermuda. It was fancy and she was flying to New York all the time. Then she landed a job at a multibillion-dollar hedge fund in London. But after a divorce, she reevaluated her life. She had a successful career and was doing what she was "supposed" to be doing, but wasn't feeling fulfilled. As she describes it, "Nothing was wrong, exactly. It just felt blah." One day, a friend introduced her to a blog about financial freedom and early retirement. Kerri was hooked. She started independently studying books and blogs about living off passive income and lifestyle design. The light bulb went off for her and she set her goal to become financially free. Kerri worked on her money mindset, altered her habits, and spent more consciously. She strategized, made more spreadsheets, and saved. Kerri became a self-made millionaire this way. Now she works as a money coach. Yes, Kerri was formally trained in the world of business finance, but personal finance is her true gift. She studied on her own, mastered it in her own life, and is now teaching others how to do it too. If Kerri had focused only on what she went to school for, then she'd still be stuck working at that billion-dollar hedge fund. But when she focuses on her natural gifts and what excites her? She's coaching clients on her laptop, beside the lake at her Canadian cottage. And when it gets chilly, she's spending months in Mexico, where she's surfing at sunrise.

Now, it's your turn:

What are you good at that nobody taught you how to do? Write down five—even ten—things that you intuitively know how to do. (And if you have more, keep going.)

chapter 5

What Have You Been Unexpectedly Criticized For?

Have you ever been taken aback by someone's harsh comments and thought, *Where the hell did that come from?* You may have been especially upset if you gave your best effort and somehow *still* fell short.

When someone pops your tires entirely out of the blue, then you can wind up perceiving your gifts as a weakness. Despite what that shithead said to you, this is actually a great place to take note of your brilliance.

In tenth grade I had a crush on this brown-eyed guy in my gym class. (God, why does it always start like this?) And my English teacher asked us to draft a creative essay. I can't remember what the topic was, but I decided to channel my teenage angst and hormones into this paper. I wrote this whole story about how my crush and I kept making eye contact through the bookshelves of the school library. It was about our unrequited love even though he would be moving back to Israel after graduation. I thought it would be cool if every sentence had a fruit, or sweet, or candy metaphor in it. Things like "his eyes were like chocolate-dipped almonds" or "walking home under candy-colored skies." I thought this thing was a work of art and perhaps my best writing all year.

A few weeks later, the teacher gave us our grades. My best friend, who was sitting across from me, got her essay back. She smiled and said she scored a ninety-something.

I got mine back, but there wasn't a number at the top of the page like on everyone else's.

There were words.

They said, "Um . . . we need to talk about this."

Are you freaking kidding me? I worked so hard on this! This was so creative! This was my art!

When we talked, my teacher said my essay was "too creative" and too "out there."

For my whole life, I had prided myself on making things that came from my imagination. I made outfits for all my dolls. I learned how to use the sewing machine on my own and made a stuffed moose (how Canadian) that legitimately looked store-bought. I even sewed my own bathing suit without a pattern. (Side note: It didn't cover my boobs entirely. And side boob wasn't in back then.)

But this day in tenth grade was the day I told myself I was *not* creative. I actually felt stupid for thinking that this was a strength of mine because, clearly, Ms. Brown hated my work. Plus, this was Advanced Placement English, and if my teacher didn't like this, then I guess it wasn't good.

I told myself:

Don't write this kind of stuff.
Just give her what she wants and you'll get a good grade.
Stick to the rules.
Be more like your peers.
Don't stand out too much.

*You need to do well in this class, so drop the weird stuff and get the
job done.*

When people unexpectedly criticize you, they just might be pointing in the direction of your genius.

Let me give you some more examples.

My college career counselor said straight up, "Kelly, you're too enthusiastic."

Look, I might be "too enthusiastic" to work at a desk job, but if she thought more creatively (and maybe did her job properly), she might have turned that gift toward something like sales or leadership, where you have to be all rah-rah-rah, or entrepreneurship, for heaven's sake. Do you know how enthusiastic you have to be to get a business off the ground? Do you know how enthusiastic you have to be to get your first sale? You have to be so excited that you make *other* people excited. And excited enough that they pull out a credit card and spend their after-tax dollars on your stuff.

But little eighteen-year-old me trusted her. I took her words as truth and looked at my blessing as a curse. Point taken, I simmered down and got quieter. I didn't crack my usual jokes, I held myself back from getting too excited, and I tried to be all buttoned-up and professional.

I told myself:

Be quieter.
Don't draw attention to yourself.
Don't laugh too loud. People are staring.
*Be more like Alice. She already got her full-time offer and she's what
employers are looking for. She's sweet, she's nice, she's more level-
headed. Act like her.*

One potential employer told me my interests were "too basic" and my résumé was "too much" because I put photos on it and incorporated color. She literally told me, "You weren't our first pick, but the first, second, third,

and fourth person on our list have all declined, so we're offering it to you."
Jeez, my résumé must have been really bad for me to be the fifth pick.

I told myself:

Stop trying to be creative. It's not working.
You're not standing out—you're just making yourself look dumb.
Just fit in for once, okay?

And it doesn't end there.

People have criticized me for being "too unrealistic." I have big, wild,
crazy ideas. Many, actually. Being realistic sounds boring. I'm a visionary.
But I also got unexpectedly criticized for saying that. One dude in Silicon
Valley told me that I shouldn't call myself a visionary because that makes
me sound like I have a big ego. He said, "It's okay if other people call you
a visionary, but you can't say that about yourself." He went out of his
way to give me this unsolicited advice. (And we all know that unsolicited
advice is the worst.)

This is what I know for sure: the more you express your authentic self,
the more you'll connect with what you'll deeply desire. Too creative, too
enthusiastic, too much of a visionary, too unrealistic . . . Well, that sounds
like the making of a genius to me.

Here are a few things to reflect on:

- When have people said you are "too much" or "too
  _____"? Recall times in your life when you were
  shocked at someone's response to your best efforts.
- What are five qualities that you've been unexpectedly criticized for? Write them down. Now, notice if
  these are actually your gifts.

chapter 6

What's Something Easy for You Where You See Others Struggle?

Let me tell you about the easiest class I ever took: public speaking.

It was one of those total "joke" classes and a GPA booster cuz lord knows I was bound to get an A. Every week, students gave a speech at the front of the class. While I rolled outta bed, brainstormed a half-assed speech on the bus, and finished it on the spot in front of everyone in the 9 a.m. class, *the other kids struggled.* Blue, collared shirts now featured huge pit stains and folks dabbed their foreheads with tissues to stop the water springs pouring from their hairline.

I realized, *Oh, this isn't easy for everyone.*

I never knew that speaking was a gift for me. But when I saw how much other kids were preparing for their presentations, I was like, *Wait . . . maybe I am good at this?*

An easy way to spot your hidden gifts is by noticing what you excel at, what you can do on the spot and hardly have to prepare for, while you see others scrambling like crazy 'n' sweating balls. Chances are, you can do this quickly too. You can get it done, with almost no thought.

So, what's stupidly simple for you? What's something that you could just show up and totally nail? Where can you wing it with confidence? What can you turn around in no time? These are very obvious places to spot your gifts.

Write it down:

- What's something easy for you, but that you notice others struggle to do? Reflect on times in your life when you, too, had the "Oh shit, I'm good at this!" moment. Write them down.
- Write down five things that you can do really quickly. As in, with almost no thought or preparation.

chapter 7

How Is Your Darkest Shadow Your Greatest Gift?

If a good friend said something scathing about you behind your back, what are the three worst words they could use to describe you? The words that make you wince the most and illuminate your shadow since they represent the side of you that you unconsciously hide, are ashamed of, and try to cover up. The concept of shadow was created by psychoanalyst Carl Jung.

For me, those three words are *fake*, *fraud*, and *liar*.

Am I a fake, a fraud, and a liar? Well, I sure used to think so. Then I learned that this was my impostor syndrome and inner critic saying, *Who are you to do this? Don't you think you should be farther along by now? If you were more accomplished, then people would take you more seriously.* Turns out, I was scoring myself on the wrong grading system.

So here's what you need to know: the opposite of your shadow can showcase your most genuine gifts. The darkness is the light if you look at it another way.

For example, I'd be pissed if a newspaper said I was fake. As in, the flavor of fake that is scripted, is reality TV ready, and has too much Botox. I loathe people who avoid vulnerability, wear an everything-is-great mask, and wanna small-talk about the weather. Hmmm, where does this stem from? This is very embarrassing to admit, but growing up, I always wanted to be cool. I'd ask my mom to highlight my hair with bleach to look like the popular girls, I wore the blue eye-shadow in the '90s, and I made sure that my hoodie said "Abercrombie" on it. But because I knew I was trying so hard to be cool, I felt super fake.

When we have a trait that we really don't like in ourselves or others, it's a good idea to flip this around on its head and see if there is a gift on the other side. The opposite of fake is real. And if I look for areas in my life where I'm real, I notice a genuine gift for authenticity and vulnerability. Sometimes, we're just staring at the wrong thing. For example, I've made a habit out of sharing the honest journey, not just the Instagram-filtered version, and I try to show up as my authentic self in all areas of life. I mean, in my podcast I openly talk about business failures that made me cry so hard I had ribbons of snot running down my cheek. (Sexy!) Instead of focusing on my fear of being fake, I should really look at my gift of being real.

Another shadowy aspect of myself that I held onto for years was that I was a fraud. There was a teensy part of me that always said, *Are you really licensed to do this? Shouldn't you have* more *experience? Are you truly qualified to give people advice?* You see, lying and cheating drive me nuts. And part of me worried that I was the biggest liar in town. Feeling this way actually held me back from being more visible and helping more people, because I was just waiting for someone to spot my inadequacy. If my business was having a hard month, I'd feel like a fraud for telling other people how to run theirs. If I was having a breakdown and started wondering if winning the lottery—or, dare I say, looking for a job—would be easier, I'd feel like a fraud for not having it all together. Plus, unlike other coaches, I didn't achieve my success super fast. It wasn't overnight. I've done well in my corner of the internet, but I'm not a household name. ("Uh, Kelly Trach who? Trach, as in rhymes with scratch? Trash . . . like the garbage? Track with a *k*? Oh! Kelly T-R-A-C-H! Yeah . . . I've never heard of her.")

I've never made a million dollars in a day like other people on Instagram do. And I don't have a private jet. I fly economy, I absolutely love a good two-for-one coupon, and my designer handbag is secondhand. I currently have about two thousand followers on Instagram, and when I leave a hotel room, I take the extra bags of tea. I'm not exactly the image of success: I am young, I was previously very entrepreneurially unlucky, and I've been slow to succeed and get my shit together.

When I flip this shadowy trait around, integrity is on the other side. Then I ask myself, *How could I have the gift of integrity instead?*

I can answer that quickly. (1) It's always been paramount that I walk the walk, not just talk the talk. Everything I teach is what I actually do. (2) I'd never be the entrepreneur who poses with their buddy's yellow Lamborghini because I want you to think it's mine. (3) I'm a big believer in karma, so I don't take organic quinoa from the bulk bins and number it as the regular quinoa to save myself a couple of bucks at Whole Foods. (4) I show up for clients right on time, pay back the friend that lent me twenty bucks, and deliver on my promises. I even have my own working definition of integrity, which is, "I do what I say I'm going to do by when I say I'm going to do it."

When I recognized my gift of integrity, it helped me let go of my worry that I was one big disingenuous fraud and see myself as a human who was just trying her best.

And hey, perhaps the thing that you have been running away from your whole life is the thing that makes you the most successful. I spent years trying to run away from being a fake, a fraud, and a liar. I thought that if I just got enough awards and accolades, then I'd feel better about myself and people would never have the chance to "figure me out." Unconsciously, my shadows propelled me to achieve. Turns out, my vulnerability and integrity were gifts that were sitting just on the other side. I only wish I'd noticed these sooner.

Here are some questions to answer:

- If a good friend said something scathing about you behind your back, what are the three worst words they could use to describe you? List them.
- What qualities do you hate in other people? What traits drive you bonkers? Really piss you off? Get you in a tizzy? Get you all riled up? Write them down.
- Based on everything you've written, how could the flip sides of these traits you loathe be an indication of your gifts? What's the opposite of your shadows? What's your light on the other side of the darkness?
- What deep, dark fear has actually fueled your entire quest? And can you come to peace with it? Maybe even thank it?

chapter 8

What Do People Come to You For?

What advice do you find yourself always giving? What do friends want to learn from you? What do peeps ask you at parties when you meet them? "Oh! You do roofing? We have a leak . . . Any input?"

People come to you because they see you as an expert in this space and want guidance. They already see your gifts, so you need to see 'em for yourself.

For example, everyone wants to talk to me when their life is falling apart or they are on the brink of a breakthrough. Generally speaking, these events happen at the same time, so don't panic if you find yourself in this pickle.

"Kelly, I hate my job and I can't do it anymore. What should I do?"
"Kelly, things are not working out. I want to quit. What advice
     do you have?"

"Kelly, I have three opportunities on the table. Which one
    should I take?"

"Kelly, I need your advice on starting my own thing. What is
    my next step?"

If you're anything like me, people ask me the same shit over and over
again. (Which is why I got into the online education business, BTW.)
The questions that come my way all have the same underlying theme:
people standing at a fork in the road and wondering if they should take
the road less traveled.

Look at what's getting reflected to you. What is the number one
question you get asked? What do old friends send you random Facebook
messages about? "Hey, Kelly, long time no chat! I see you are doing business coaching now . . . Can I ask you a question about how you got
started? Thanks in advance . . ."

And hey, this is not just what people come to you for, but what you
love talking about.

What topics turn you on? What could you chat about until 2 a.m.?
What things will make you want to stay on the phone with a friend for
far too long, even though you really have to pee but the conversation is
too good to end?

If people come to you for it, *and* you love talking about it, this is a
good indicator of your gifts.

Why?

Because you'll always be drawn to your genius. It's like the universe
has a big neon arrow sign pointing to it and saying, "For heaven's sake,
look here!" You know, the kind they have at fast-food drive-throughs that
lure you in for a cola and an ice cream cone late at night. Repeating topics
and recurring themes are the universe's way of trying to get your attention
because it's what you're meant to be doing.

Answer these questions to uncover more innate gifts:

- What advice do you find yourself always giving?
- What are people already coming to you for?
- What is the number one question you get asked?
- What problems are you solving?
- What type of "friend" are you in your group? The good listener? The careerist? The hostess with the mostest? The wingman? This is another place to check for any innate gifts because you're already expressing them naturally within your peer group.
- What topics could you chat about late into the night?
- Based on all of this, are there any recurring topics? Take out your magnifying glass and do some detective work to look for parallel themes here.

chapter 9

What Have You Been Unconsciously Doing for a Long Time?

My very first job was as a slide attendant at the local pool, where I would sit at the top of the slide. (In a very sexy yellow pinny, if I may add, that said "Slide Attendant" in huge obnoxious letters.) I would tell kids "Okay, go!" when it was their turn for, like, two hours straight. I got this job so I could work my way up at the pool by getting on the staff's radar; I was hoping that they'd hire me later as a lifeguard and swim instructor. My plan worked because I got the gig.

I've been in teaching roles since I was legal working age in Canada. I taught swimming lessons for six years. I taught the babysitter's class. (I hated babysitting but loved teaching the class.) I tutored kids at my parents' kitchen table in high school. I tutored young kids, old kids, and kids with special needs. People came to me because I taught things in different ways; used visuals, toys, and colors; and catered to each student's learning style. I was a teaching assistant in high school. I was a teaching assistant twice in university. I taught tutorials three times a week to my 150 students. I loved teaching. So much. And it is no surprise that my whole work now is teaching. Teaching clients, teaching courses, teaching in my podcast, and now teaching you in this book.

Teaching was easy for me, but I wrote it off because it wasn't hard. (Cuz, you know, I should be doing something like finding a cure for cancer, right?)

Despite conventional wisdom, what you consider to be "too easy" is actually the no-brainer work you should be pursuing.

We're going for that natural, easy, fluid feeling. Now, you might be thinking, *But, Kelly, I want to challenge myself.* Look, I get it. You can still be rooted in your gifts *and* challenge yourself. The key is not to just think bigger = better. It's about creating more space and time to do your genius. For example, if you're gifted at career coaching and work at the local college, perhaps your goal is to start a side hustle where you can book additional clients after hours. That way, you could help more soon-to-be grads and generate more opportunity to be in your genius. If you're a young law student, pull an Elle Woods and see how you can challenge yourself to volunteer on a big case. If you're a student with a gift for politics and a passion for environmentalism, push yourself to score an internship on an eco-conscious campaign team that you wanna get behind. We're aiming for intentional goals that amplify your genius, not drain it. It's all soul, no hamster wheel.

To figure out your no-brainer career, take inventory of what you have been doing consciously (or unconsciously) for a long time. Our greatest gifts are generally right under our nose. It's so glaringly obvious to others, but we can't see it ourselves.

The best way to start is by looking at your past work experience. What kinds of jobs have you had? It's important to take note of what you've been doing for a long time, what roles you've been drawn to, and what skill sets you've been developing. You might not be aware that you've been mastering your craft for a while now. So write down all the odd jobs, random internships, and volunteer work you've done. Now, are there any collective themes that surface when you evaluate them as a whole? Perhaps you'll notice that they have all been analytical roles or that they have all been jobs for which you need to be a people person.

Your past work experiences are a gold mine for your gifts. Even if your résumé has been totally random, I bet there are some subtle nuances that you can pull out and decipher. Maybe you'll think, *Based on all these jobs, I guess I'm just really open to adventure.*

You have been unconsciously honing and mastering your craft for a long time now. The key thing here is to recognize the power your experience holds. Many clients come to me and worry that they don't have enough experience to do their genius as their work now. The secret is knowing how to properly position your experience and make it relevant to the work you're doing.

Here's my framework you can use on your website, in cover letters and interviews, or any other time you need to convey your value to others. This way of articulating your value is especially useful if you have experience that doesn't feel cohesive, are multi-passionate with many interests, took a gap year, or even had a failure (or three).

Here's how you can position it:

Because I [did X past job], I learned how to [do Y certain skill set]. Now, I can [help you achieve Z desired outcome] because of it.

Here are my examples:

Because I worked at Tesla selling $100,000 cars, I learned how to help people make a major buying decision by asking thoughtful questions to ensure that the vehicle met their needs. Now, I can teach you *how to sell your $1,000 consulting packages in a way that's based on listening and exploring your clients' needs, rather than pushing and convincing.*

Because I've been in teaching roles for the last eleven years, I learned how to communicate in a clear, simple, step-by-step way and teach anything to anybody. Now, I can teach you how to build a digital business in a proven process from A to Z because of it.

Because I've had three failed businesses, I learned how to properly validate my ideas and ensure that I'm only pouring resources into what's actually going to work. Now, I can help you validate your business idea to see if it will be successful before you invest a penny or lift a finger to start it.

See the difference when I frame it like that?

Here's a real-world interview example. Joanna worked at Uber in operations. This is a great job for someone with a business background, which she had. She wanted to switch departments and get into product management. Usually, this is a job for software engineers, which she wasn't. In her interview, this is what she said to land the gig:

Because I had an operations role, I learned how to experiment and launch so that drivers can be optimally placed at the right time relative to our customers. While I was in the role, I found that A/B testing was good for building an app, but what was even better was going to the customers, hearing the user stories directly, and translating that into app improvements. Since I oversaw many global cities, I learned that you can't just build software in a vacuum because customers have different needs. I also learned how to forecast, predict, and understand the algorithm. Now, with my hands-on experience overseeing operations, I can step into this new role.

This worked well for Joanna because she found the one advantage she had over all the other applicants: a different approach to app improvements through customer feedback coupled with prior experience at the company. She also knew that her lack of software engineering education would be a point of tension going into the interview, so she gathered ahead of time the reasons why she could rise to the occasion in the role. Next time you have to showcase your expertise to a potential employer or customer, use this framework to cover your blind spots.

Great, now it's your turn:

- Write down all the jobs, internships, part-time gigs, and volunteer positions you've had. Yep, everything.
- Now, are there any collective themes that surface when you evaluate them as a whole? Take note of any that emerge.
- How can you write your experience in a way that reflects your expertise? Use my framework.

Because I [did X past job], I learned how to [do Y certain skill set]. Now, I can [help you achieve Z desired outcome] because of it.

chapter 10

What's Your Favorite Way to Fill an Empty Sunday?

What are my hobbies?

As my friend bluntly pointed out during my last year of university, "Kelly, you don't have any hobbies."

Oh.

We live in a world where we are busy, busy, busy. And you're not alone if you can't think of three pastimes you enjoy, because your life is full or because you've lost touch with yourself. I've been there too. Plus, it's okay if your hobbies aren't bougie, like knowing all the wine pairings, or hyper-specific, like studying Egyptian hieroglyphics.

An easy entry point to this question is, If you had an empty Sunday, what would be your favorite way to fill it?

If I had a spare Sunday, I'd ideally do the following: I'd make pancakes, then go for heated vinyasa, and actually wash my hair when I'm done (instead of using dry shampoo for the seventh time that week) and put on makeup. Next, I'd catch up with a friend for a coffee and talk about life, our goals, and big ideas. In the late afternoon, I'd go for a walk by the ocean and listen to a podcast. Then, I'd finish up the night by cooking a new vegan recipe I found on Pinterest that wouldn't turn out as pretty as the picture, but I'd try my best.

If you are gifted at something, you'll find yourself doing it all the time. This is why I pose this question to all my clients, even though it sounds as serious as something you'd find in a multiple-choice magazine quiz. Your answer provides a lot of insight into who you are as a person, your values, your gifts, and what kind of career you could create. How you respond also reveals the core essence of who you really are. It's not about what you do for work or where you went to school, but about your real self. (Which is where all the magic happens anyway.) Because on a lazy Sunday, nobody is watching and you can drop the pretenses. You can swap out that dry-clean-only blazer for your jammies. Because Sunday is usually about recharging for the week ahead, it's also a good place to look for which activities give you more energy when you do them, where you find flow, and what you never get tired of doing. Recognizing what energizes you is essential for finding your genius.

As you comb through my example, you'll notice that making things (making pancakes, doing my makeup, and trying a Pinterest recipe) and connecting with people (catching up with a friend and listening to a podcast) are two common themes. So I want you to think about your ideal Sunday.

Now that we've covered what you do with your spare time, let's assess what you do with your spare change. What do you spend your dough on for fun? Maybe it's vintage Creamsicle-colored electric guitars. Silent retreats. The churros at Disneyland. Whatever it is for you.

Take note of what you'll gleefully swipe your credit card for and list five things. Then consider why you feel this way about those particular things. Ask yourself: Which of my gifts is presenting itself here? Write anything that comes to mind.

Here's my example:

I love to spend money on dinners and coffees with friends. Why? I love to connect with people and socialize. What gift is presenting itself here? Maybe connecting, socializing, talking, and relating to others.

I love to spend money on nourishing food and whatever new trendy sauces, spreads, and jams are at the store. Why? I love to try new recipes and see if I can make something tasty. What gift is presenting itself here? Getting creative. Making something new. Being spontaneous. Innovating. I also love a good logo and packaging. So maybe this has to do with being creative again?

I love to spend money on new clothes and a good thrift-store find. Why? I love putting together outfits. I love design and style. I love anything visually striking. I also love finding something old at the thrift store and making it new again. What gift is presenting itself here? Being creative again, I guess. And creating.

I love to spend money on good books and online courses. Why? I love learning—especially from mentors who I consider to be masters of their craft. When I learn from the master, it helps me hone my craft even more. What gift is presenting itself here? Teaching and learning.

I love to spend money on trips to Hawaii. Why? I love the time to get quiet, listen to myself, and take a break from the noise of the world. What gift is presenting itself here? Being still and going within. Listening to my own inner voice and intuition. The gift at work here is connecting, even if I'm doing so with myself instead of others. Connecting with myself ultimately helps me connect deeper with people when I come back from vacation because I can be really present with clients and truly hear them.

By uncovering overlapping themes in your pastimes and credit card statements, you'll likely spot a gift or two.

Questions for reflection:

- If you had an open Sunday, how would you fill your time?
- What activities create more energy for you in your life when you do them?
- Where do you find flow?
- What kinds of activities did you gravitate toward as a kid?
- What do you never get tired of doing?
- What brings you great pleasure when you spend money on it? List five things. Consider why you feel this way about those particular things. Then ask yourself: What gift is presenting itself here? Write down any gifts that come to mind.

chapter 11

What Does Your Bookshelf Say About You?

Okay, I know this chapter sounds like a cheesy phrase on the front cover of a girl's teen magazine, but bear with me.

What's on your bookshelf? Take a hot second and peruse your book collection, or e-reader, if you're fancy like that.

What kinds of books are on your bookshelf? What are you deeply interested in? What topics and theories do you love to explore? Look for themes here. Is it anime? Self-help? Vampire-based fiction?

Now, here's the real question: What do any common themes say about your gifts and authentic desires?

Let's look at the example of Rosie. She's got engineering textbooks still kicking around from college, cute comic books, and everything ever penned by Marie Kondo. Her bookshelf reflects her gifts of having an artistic eye (which comes from the comic books), being ridiculously intentional (à la Marie Kondo), and being a critical thinker with a flair for the details (you guessed right—the textbooks).

My bookshelf is essentially a blend of spirituality and moneymaking. (And yes, those two can harmoniously exist.) With books like *Feng Shui and Money*, *Secrets of the Millionaire Mind*, *The Seven Spiritual Laws of Success*, *Daring Greatly*, and *The Universe Has Your Back*, there is an overall theme of going for what you really want in life and making money doing it.

Now, I want you to identify your three favorite books of all time. (I know, it's hard.) For me, it's Danielle LaPorte's *The Desire Map*, Jen Sincero's *You Are a Badass at Making Money*, and Brené Brown's *The Gifts of Imperfection*. Their core themes, respectively, are how to pursue goals with soul, how to master the mindset of wealth, and how to let go of who you think you're supposed to be so that you can embrace who you are. (I literally wrote their subtitles down here for you.)

You don't have to look hard to see that what I ultimately do (and sell) is a blend of these three books. Essentially, my business boils down to these questions:

- What's your dream?
- How can you make money doing your dream?
- How can you show up as your real self while you do it?

You'll always be influenced and inspired by the people who reflect your own gifts. It's going to be subtle, like the pull of the moon's force on the tide. But you gotta understand that your bookshelf is really just holding up a mirror and reflecting back to you what work you should be doing in the world.

So, what is your bookshelf telling you? What can you infer from those past purchases and ink-stained pages?

Take these questions for a spin:

- What kinds of books are on your bookshelf? What are you deeply interested in? What topics and theories do you love to explore?

- How is your own ability being reflected back to you on your bookshelf? Remember, you'll always subconsciously gravitate to your own genius and be mesmerized by the people who already possess it.

- What are your three favorite books? When you evaluate them as a whole, what do these books say about you as a person? What can you infer about your own gifts here?

chapter 12

What Are You Great at That You Talk Yourself Out of Doing?

And yes, I mean *that* thing that's been in your heart for a while. Yet you keep saying, "I can't," or "I'm not really that great." And despite doing all the journal prompts in this book, perhaps you still look at your notebook and think *nahhhh*.

Here's what you need to know: **Your undying dream is what contains your deepest genius. It contains the deepest exploration of your own heart. It might be unbeknownst to you, but the thing that calls to you in the middle of the night just might be what you're here to do. In fact, chosen to do. By a power greater than you. And if you aren't all into that spiritual mumbo jumbo, then I guess you could say it's simply the pursuit of a lifetime.**

There's a boatload of gifts orbiting that dream. Think about which gifts of yours would become so glaringly obvious if you stepped into your highest vision and deepest calling. Look, I'm not saying you have to *do* it right now. I'm just saying you should *think* about it. Your goal will have that *holy-shit-balls-this-is-scary* element, so I want you to take the pressure off and get back into dreaming. See the version of yourself that you'd step into. Witness your own potential. Bask in the highest dimension of your being.

Every time you get scared or nervous, know this: **Your most sacred ambitions are the ones that are aligned with your highest expression of genius.**

Let me show you an example of how this works. Here's a conversation I had with my pal Olivia, a sixth-grade elementary school teacher:

Olivia, visualize and tell me your dream. *"My biggest dream is to be a good teacher and actively know I'm making a difference in my students' lives. I'd like to have the kind of impact where students come back to you when they are adults and say that you changed their life."*

Olivia, what are you great at that you talk yourself *out* of doing? *"Well, everyone tells me that I'm a good teacher, but I don't know if that's true. People tell me I have a gift for teaching and I jokingly say, 'Ahhh! Shut up! Stop talking!' It comes from a lack of self-confidence. Sometimes people see my abilities better than I can. The perfectionist within me always wants my work to be better. Even when people say my work is great, I'm always like, 'It's not good enough; I can always do better.'"*

Olivia, let's fast-forward thirty years and pretend you ran into a student in the supermarket and they told you that you changed their life. What kind of gifts and talents would you have really honed if you were that kind of teacher? *"Helping kids bring out their own gifts. Helping them find their path. Being a leader."*

What skill sets would you intuitively tap into? *"Being a good communicator, listening to others, and bringing out the best in people."*

I've known Olivia since childhood and I'm totally not surprised that she's getting great feedback at work. She's always been stellar at teaching, listening, and bringing out the best in others. Want the kicker? Olivia is great at all of those gifts now. Which means ditto for you.

Answer these questions:

- What long-held dream do you have tucked inside your heart that you keep second-guessing?
- What current talents would you harness if you were to live out your dream? What skill sets would you intuitively tap into? What traits would automatically come out to play?
- If you pursued your dream, what hidden gifts would reveal themselves?

Part 2

How to Find Your Genius

By now, you should have a long list of gifts from all the exercises in part one. That is, unless you are just skimming and haven't done shit. In that case, I can't help ya. But if you've been following along, now it's time to use the work you've done to discover your gifts and find your genius.

chapter 13

What's the Red Thread That's Been Weaving Your Whole Life?

I've had a weird journey. I've had many random jobs and I feel like I've lived many lifetimes. For eons, I felt like the odd duck out. While other people had a "normal" career path, I felt like I was a hot mess of random experiences that were glued together like a fifth-grade art assignment bedazzled with glitter and googly eyes. I've started many things but haven't finished most of them. I've had dozens of semi-started businesses, like a fashionable rain jacket brand and a line of fiber cookies. I've sold content ranging from cookbooks to coaching packages. I've tried everything from acting to being a law firm receptionist. I've made money flipping things on Craigslist, making balloon animals for kids, and emceeing violin performances.

I wrote off all these seemingly random pursuits as "one more stupid thing Kelly tried . . . that didn't work out."

I used to beat myself up for being a flake and a failure. I felt like I was wasting my life while my best friend was working at a swanky company's Santa Monica office where she had a solid career trajectory, a serious salary, access to office surfboards, *and a new promotion.*

When I started my coaching business, I stopped feeling like a flake.

My gifts of speaking, teaching, creating, and connecting all cosmically combined to give me the exact, right ingredients to build a unique business and to be the right woman for the job. Everything I learned in those previous roles strangely combined into all the lessons I needed to prepare me for this point in my journey.

Every talent and trait I needed to do my genius was something I picked up along the way.

Lifeguarding taught me how to stay calm under pressure and keep a level head when shit hits the fan.

Flipping stuff on Craigslist taught me how to market, position, and sell things online to strangers.

Musical theater taught me how to speak on stages and entertain people in my podcast.

Taking people for coffee in business school to ask them questions about their career lent a hand when I needed to interview podcast guests.

Writing for a magazine helped me hone my voice.

Business case competitions taught me how to spot the problems in a company and find a solution in under one hour, which prepared me for doing something similar with real clients.

Tutoring kids who were flunking classes taught me how to be a good teacher, which helped me when it came time to create my own courses.

Being terrible at math taught me how to sharpen my intuition so that I could make decisions in other ways.

No matter how random your journey has been, you've arrived here with the exact tools in your toolbox to build a career, business, or side hustle based on your genius. I call this your "red thread," and it's been weaving your genius together throughout your life. It's not by accident. It's intentional.

If you've ever tried to sew a garment, then you know it starts by cutting out peculiar-looking pieces from cloth. One by one, you stitch them together. For a while, it looks like "WTF is this?" And you think, *Oh my god, am I screwing this up? Did I make a misstep? I totally fucked up the pattern.* In the middle of the project, it looks like you just wasted three hours of your life that you'll never get back. Then, as you get closer to the final result, you start to see the shape of the garment and, looking back, you realize it all makes sense now. Life has a way of working like this. Your red thread makes sense of all the odds 'n' ends in your past experiences. Everything that you've done has taught you the precise things required for you to do your genius now.

You don't need more work experience or another certification when you realize that you've got a red thread that's been weaving your gifts together all along. So ditch the fear that you're not experienced enough, and let go of feeling like you must acquire more. Your past is peppered with strands of your genius.

So I want you to look back on all your past work experiences, key turning points in your life, and moments that taught you certain skill sets or ways of seeing the world. I also want you to include the harder parts of your life and how those have informed your genius. Also include random things you garnered from your upbringing and surroundings, and write down what you learned from those early years. That way, you'll find the red thread in your own life.

I find my red thread theory to be even more true for those of us who don't have traditional work experience or a cohesive résumé. Realize that even the failures, the stuff that didn't go anywhere, and the stupid attempts (especially those) have all taught you something you needed to know. They probably taught you more than you'll ever realize. Your destiny is defined by those fork-in-the-road moments. And your red thread only grows stronger through times of dark, unbearable pain.

It's really important when you see it like this:

If I had never [done X specific thing], then I would have never learned how to [Y outcome], which I really needed in order to pursue my genius.

If I had never taken the leap to study abroad in Paris, then I would have never realized that there was a life calling my name outside the corporate hamster wheel that business school was preparing me for.

If I had never quit that full-time job, then I would have never moved to San Francisco, which set me on my authentic path.

If I had never launched three start-ups that all crashed and burned, then I'd have never known how to take risks, which helped me reach a point in my life when I could give up my ego, stop trying to look good on paper, and intentionally just "do what I was good at."

If I had never lost a lot of money, my apartment, and almost my whole business in a bad business deal, then I would have never learned how to trust my own wisdom.

If I had never failed at publishing my first book, then I would have never known how to pitch this one when it mattered the most.

Getting off track is how you find your truth, so you have to trust the cosmic plan for your life. You have to trust that the universe is taking you to a better place than you could ever expect, prepare for, or imagine. The best way to do this is by remembering the red thread concept when the road gets rough and the drive gets bumpy.

If you've been worrying that you're in the wrong job or feel disheartened because you can't get the one you want, just know that whatever you are doing now is teaching you something that you'll need later. **Even when you feel behind, you are right on time.** The universe is never late.

Everything that you've done, no matter how seemingly random, has brought you to this point in your destiny where you are designed to do your genius.

chapter 14

How Do Your Gifts Generate Your Genius?

STEP 1: Write down all your gifts.

Based on what you've uncovered so far, make a long list of all your gifts. Write down anything you've uncovered through the exercises in part one.

STEP 2: Look for common themes.

Pour over the list of your gifts and look for common themes. What stands out to you? What's really obvious here? Maybe you notice that you frequently mention being a good listener along with your analytical skills. Repetition is good because the recurring traits are the pulse of your genius.

I know that "looking for common themes" feels eye-roll-esque and like something annoying your high school English teacher would say as he assigned you to read *Hamlet*. Yet this step is significant. If I were coaching you, I'd be looking for patterns in your answers and listening for what's coming up frequently when we speak. So look at your list and highlight words and ideas that repeat. Just as you had to find the themes to pass high school English, you need to find the themes to discover your genius.

STEP 3: Group 'em together.

If you have gifts that can be grouped together under an overarching category, do it. Our goal here is to whittle down this list to between three and five distinctive categories. This is very important: each category needs to be different. You want the categories to sit separately like drawers in a dresser.

You'll be able to group a lot of your gifts together. When I'm working with a client, they usually have a few predominant gifts that are expressed in a multitude of ways. So if you felt like your answers to the ten questions in part one of this book were repetitive, that's a good thing.

Additionally, your categories may make sense only to you. For example, perhaps your love for taking color-coded notes is something you wanna tuck into the bucket of listening. For someone else, maybe that trait is about learning, but in your life, it represents your listening skills. Nobody is looking at your paper here, and this is not a test. There are no wrong answers. The only right answers are the ones that feel true for you.

If you have stragglers that don't make it into a category, that's okay too. Let them sit it out. If you feel like you can't part ways with them, ask yourself: What is this gift really about? Then see if it can get nestled in a drawer. Lastly, this is a good time to chuck stuff out and strike through anything that feels random.

STEP 4: Aim for three to five categories.

By now, you should have a few main categories. For example, maybe you have one category that encompasses your listening skills, one for your analytical traits, and one that's about your wickedly good brainstorming abilities.

If you have more than five, don't sweat it. Five or less makes this whole exercise easier for you, but if you have seven and literally can't let go of two, then that's fine.

Here are some examples of what your categories could look like:

- Sales, investing, listening, patience
- Seeing patterns, asking good questions, strategic thinking
- Speaking up, social justice, caring, helping others
- Creative problem solving, artistic ability, being detail-oriented

STEP 5: Pick a word to describe this category. This will be your gift.

Now, pick a word that best summarizes each category.

For example, I have gifts in marketing, making things, and creating stuff. I am gifted at dreaming and believing in possibility. I place all of these gifts in the category of "creating."

When you're categorizing a group of gifts, pick the words that feel most resonant in your body. The ones that make your heart leap out of your chest and say, "Yes! That's it!" I could use a word like *entrepreneurial*, but to me *creating* feels more like home. Go for what feels good.

STEP 6: Define the meaning of each gift.

Next, define what each gift means to you in your own words. Don't be tempted to look at a dictionary here for the definition. Look for answers inside yourself rather than beyond. This is a matter of the heart and what you know to be true.

I'll go first.

Teaching: I can teach anything to anybody. I can break down the biggest, most complex stuff into something so easy that a sixth-grader can understand it. What I teach is clear, it's concise, and it's insanely step-by-step.

Creating: I can make something out of nothing. I love making stuff—courses, podcasts, worksheets, websites. I am insanely creative and can build anything from scratch. I mean, I have dreamed up three courses, a full framework, four businesses, and a book. I've created a whole body of work out of thin air. Plus, nothing I make is "cookie-cutter." I've always run with my intuitive, scrappy, and quirky ideas. In turn, I've made a living from what I consider to be my art.

Speaking: When I speak, people listen. (I know they do because I see the podcast downloads.) Based on what my community has shared with me, they've listened to a million other people before, but when they hear it in my words, they "get it." It clicks. It resonates. It grooves with their souls and activates something deep inside their hearts. My communication style is a rare blend of vulnerability, wisdom, humor, and genuine authenticity.

Connecting: I can make friends with anyone—at any party or any bus stop. I could go to any event and walk away with five new friends. I'm your quintessential social butterfly. I also like to think I make people feel relaxed and at home with me. Like, we could kick off our shoes at a house party, sit our butts down on a comfy couch, and chat 'til midnight, covering everything from secret fears to audacious dreams to our favorite childhood books.

STEP 7: Combine your gifts.

Your genius erupts when you harness all your gifts at once and infuse them into a single endeavor. Once you settle on your top three to five gifts, I want you to look at them like a group of stars so that you can find the outline of the constellation. Our goal here is to see what kind of outcomes could be produced when we harness all your top gifts at once. Because on paper, they might look like eight random stars, but to the eye of a dreamer, they form the Big Dipper.

STEP 8: Notice how your genius shows up in everyday life.

Your genius will feel more "real" once you connect it to examples in your daily life. (It will seem less Pollyanna and more practical.) So let's get the brainstorm ball rolling. When do you harness all your gifts at once in your nine-to-five? Or in school? Or when you volunteer on Sundays? How does your genius translate into a task or express itself in an endeavor?

You might find tasks in your daily life where you're leveraging just a few gifts. For example, I'm not technically speaking as I write this (does in my head count?), but I'm leveraging my other three gifts. If I could verbally tell you all this stuff, it would be easier for me, but three outta four gifts ain't bad. Ideally, you want to aim for all of them, but doing two at once works too. You'll still find flow and create an awesome outcome.

chapter 15

You Found Your Genius, Now What?

STEP 1: Look for new possibilities to express your genius.

Do a brain dump and write down a ton of ideas for ways you can express your genius. *Don't* ask yourself: Is this a good idea? Can I make a buck doing this? Is this feasible . . . or have I just watched too many motivational videos on YouTube? It doesn't matter. For now, just write.

Notice what can be created when you combine all three to five of your gifts together. To generate as many possibilities as you can, consider the following questions:

- What could you sell, do, or make?
- How could you simply do your genius more often in your current role?
- Which companies might be hiring people with those kinds of talents? Which roles could you fill that you haven't considered before?

- What marketplace demands are met by a person with that skill set?
- Who needs your help?
- Who else has similar gifts, and what are they doing with their life? (Wink wink, nudge nudge: go back to the moneymaking exercise from chapter three about how your idols reflect your genius.)

STEP 2: Pick one possibility.

Now that you have some scribbles and chicken scratch on paper, let's talk about it.

From the list of possibilities, which one do you feel most called to pursue? What intuitively feels like the next right thing to create or do? Pick one idea that stands out to you most and develop an action plan.

For the record, I generally find that the first answer is the right one. Let me give you an example. When I was in business school, I had a red Moleskine notebook in which I brainstormed what the heck I was going to do with my life because it wasn't panning out as planned. I wrote "things I could do with my life" at the top of the page. The very first idea I wrote down was to *start a blog*. I wrote more career ideas that would let me flex my creative muscle, like working at an ad agency or joining a start-up to lead their marketing. Then I eventually came up with the inclination to *build my own tech start-up*. Look, we all know how the story ends. My start-ups sucked, I eventually came back around to the blog years later, and look where I am now. Go with what feels right the first time.

STEP 3: Outline your next steps.

Based on what you chose, here are some suggestions for what your action plan could look like.

If you want to tweak your current role so it's more tailored to your genius:

- Maybe you discover you don't need to change course entirely, and you're already doing well. If that's the case, yay! Finding your genius doesn't always require making big, life-altering changes. Rather, it can mean making little tweaks that let you do more of what you love, more often.

- Have a convo with your boss and say that you want to spend more hours working on X (your rad work that makes your genius shine) and less on Y (those soul-sucking, life-draining projects that don't leverage your gifts). Always back shit up with proof—like facts, numbers, and specific examples—where possible. If you're in your genius when doing sales, talk about how you increased revenue by 15 percent that year and how you could contribute even more to that total if you spent less time doing client onboarding.

- Talk to the person who manages your performance. That person has the most sway and feedback for you. Instead of waiting for them to talk to you, reach out first. If they aren't willing to help you create more time doing your genius, ask for additional resources, connect with a mentor at work, or speak to HR.

- Be vocal. If you have a team, tell your team what you love and how you can best contribute to your common goals. For example, maybe you want to take responsibility for research or data analysis. Speaking up about where you feel you can make the greatest impact, and exercise your genius, will benefit you and everyone you work with.

- For non-outsourceable tasks, give yourself a time limit for how long you do them. That way, you're not wallowing all day in misery, secretly crying into your coffee.

- Know your "golden hours," as I like to call them. These are the hours of the day when you are most productive. This is when you should do the tasks that align with your genius to squeeze the most juice and fulfillment out of your day. Do the other crap in your "off hours." For example, if you need to do admin, do it after lunch when you're groggy and sleepy anyway.

- Make other people respect your time more. Not everything is super urgent or requires a response ASAP, even if someone makes you feel like it. Ask yourself: How can I say no or claim more of my time so I can make room for what I care about more? Be okay with pushing back on requests, asking for more time to complete non-genius tasks, and passing politely altogether. Unless the building is on fire, nothing is urgent.

- Story time! Maria works in sales and manages three people. She was doing well and hitting all her metrics. Yet she didn't know how to say no or manage her time and other people's expectations. Getting tasks done wasn't the problem—it was the fact that she wasn't spending enough time on what was aligned with her genius. The solution? She cut *way* back on the hours she was spending answering everyone's emails so quickly. To prioritize, she now asks colleagues, "Can I get back to you on that in forty-eight hours?" and "When is the last day you need this by?" To communicate her needs, she explains that she can't turn around tasks immediately and says no frequently.

- Spend less time in meetings. Schedule and block off your time to give more attention to genius-related tasks. Say no when people request to take that time. If you're a big-time people pleaser, be honest with your manager about this trait and they will help you build confidence saying no.

- When things get busy, give yourself permission to tell people that you're feeling overwhelmed and that you need quiet time to do the tasks that exercise your genius.

If you want to find another role at your current company:

- Whose job at your company looks really neat? Could you shadow them for a day or have a meeting with them to learn more?
- When you find a cool role you're keen on, do internal informational interviews. Essentially, you channel Barbara Walters for twenty minutes and ask questions. Ask colleagues: "What traits and skill sets would I need in order to succeed in this role? Do you think I'd be good at this?" It's important to get the insider scoop and ensure that your assumptions about the role match its reality.
- Build connections with people in the department you wanna get into. Ask if anyone can share more insight about it or will mentor you to get there.
- Don't be shy about wanting to try something new. Companies want to keep good talent, so they are actually on your side. Cost-wise, it's easier to shuffle you around than it is to hire someone new and train 'em.
- My pal who's in HR says, "It makes things so much easier if you know your genius and what destination you're striving for in your career." (I did *not* pay her to say this!) Everyone can help you when *you* are clear on where you wanna go. Ask yourself: *Where do I see myself at this company in five years? What do I want to contribute?* If you give someone a clear vision, then they can nod their head in understanding and help you.

- If you have your eye on a role, showcase now the qualities that role requires. If you need to be fluent in French, hit the books. If the role requires certain metrics, like sales quotas or the number of projects you oversee, prove that you can meet them now.

- Is there a current open role that you can apply for, or can you find out if there will be one in the future? If you're already at the company, you can find that insider information. New grad Christina was doing a twenty-hour-per-week "work learn" at the local university. By simply asking her manager if new roles were opening any time soon, she scored a full-time job there. My point? Ask and ye shall receive (or at least have a better chance to).

- Talk to people who have made switches within the company and ask how they did it. Even if they are in a different field, it will be useful to hear others' stories.

If you are a soon-to-be college grad:

- Don't just look at the narrow path that college presents. Do informational interviews and invite professionals with neat jobs out for coffee. Being a student is a superpower because so many people *love* to help students; it's your main bargaining chip to get cool people to talk to you. Do your research, come prepared with a notebook and a list of questions, and write down what they say. (Taking notes will show people you're engaged and they will think you're smart. Which you are. Plus, you'll wanna look at those notes later anyway.) Send a follow-up email thanking them for their time. Also, pay for their coffee.

- If you are meeting someone at their office, ask for a tour. You'll see what different roles look like in a day-to-day setting and you'll get a vibe for the company culture. Also, if you have the chance to go

on any company tours, say yes. That way you can see where you
feel pulled to participate and where your genius feels welcomed.

- Think about the recent alumni who have secured jobs. Is there
anyone whose experience resonates with you and who has gifts
similar to yours? If so, what kind of career serves their genius?

- Don't try to be anything you're not in a job interview. If you
have to fake it at the start, then you'll be faking it forever. Interviews are a lot like dating: it's better to be yourself because it
weeds out the wrong matches quickly. I'd rather you show up in
your genius fully and get rejected than be stuck with a dud who
doesn't even realize how special you are. In interviews, let your
authentic self and genius shine. If the company doesn't give you
a call back, consider it a blessing. And if they do, then it means
they value your gifts.

- Network the crap out of your college years. Talk to career coun-
selors, go to networking events that your campus puts on, and
message people in alumni databases. Also ask your professors if
they can make any introductions on your behalf or connect you
to people for informational interviews.

If you are a high school student:

- Explore all the nifty things out there. Trial and error works fabulously, I find. Join a club, learn Japanese, or sign up for the band.

- Tour colleges and go *inside* the buildings. You can't make an
admissions choice based on how pretty the campus gardens are,
okay? In high school, I was dead set on science. Then I saw the
inside of a research lab on campus. I was like, *Nope!* Going on
campus tours can help you visualize where your genius feels
most at home.

- Be honest about your genuine interests. If you're looking to go to college or trade school, dump society's expectations and pursue what fascinates you. If you're not sure about your interests, revisit chapter eleven about what's on your bookshelf.

- Nourish your genius outside school hours. Keep doing the things where you find flow, and know that it's okay if it's not academic. If you love video games, keep playing them. One of my pals discovered that he wanted to study computer science in college because he loved them so much. For kicks, he made his own game in his dorm room. Now that game he built is his full-time job because it's super-duper popular and people buy it.

If you want to find a new job or switch careers:

- Don't just look at option A or B for a career. Get creative and brainstorm C to Z. You can do this by actively seeking out new peeps who are doing cool things in the world. Listen to podcasts where the hosts interview experts and icons in a particular field, watch YouTube videos and TED talks, and go to interesting talks in your city. This will expose you to other careers out there.

- Find others who are doing what you wanna do. Learn how they got there, watch their interviews, and study their journeys. If you can, email them (or ask a mutual pal for an introduction) and kindly ask for a quick twenty-minute phone call. Have your questions ready to go and end on time. If you want an in-person meeting, volunteer to meet them at their office with their favorite order from their favorite restaurant. Everyone's gotta eat.

- Surround yourself with ass-kickers. When I was in San Francisco, I knew, like, five people. Which meant I had to make friends and not watch Netflix alone on the couch while eating takeout. I pushed myself out of my comfort zone and went to an event every night. I looked for meetups, Facebook events, and what was happening at coworking spaces, and I said yes to every invite I got. I'd slap on a name tag, talk to strangers, and learn what they were doing. By the end of my first week, I had one job offer. By the end of the first month, I had five offers. I accepted none, but my point is that life is a fifty-fifty dance with the universe; you do half and the universe does half. Opportunities usher themselves into your life when you put yourself in scenarios where that can happen.

- If you want a job in another city, try moving there for one month. (Or one or two weeks if that's all that your vacation days allow.) Build connections, go to events every night, and meet people. If you wanna be a Hollywood starlet, try a mini-move to Los Angeles. You will create more traction there than waiting around at home, filing your nails, and waiting for the phone to ring with an invitation to go.

- Embrace bravery. All it takes is a few seconds of courage when opportunity strikes. Like, to interject into a conversation that you overheard and say, "Oh! You're hiring for that? I could help!" It's these tiny moments of courage that change the course of your life. So don't overwhelm yourself thinking you need to prep for hours to pump yourself up. It's usually about twenty seconds and it's over. The universe rewards the brave.

If you want to start a side hustle or business:

- Your genius + your deepest interest = a business you could talk about and do forever. For me, teaching + speaking + connecting + creating + entrepreneurship = fireworks. When you have a few interests, see if you can rope them together into a venture or pick the one that's best aligned with your top interest.

- A great way to identify new pursuits and business opportunities is to take note of what kinds of problems people are coming to you with. The purpose of a business is to take someone's problem and solve it. So if you are getting the same types of questions, that is a good sign that you could craft a side hustle or business around it.

- Make a big list of things you could create, do, offer, or sell based on your genius. This includes what you mentioned in chapter three when you listed how the folks you admire are making money.

- If you're looking to create a service, consider what journeys and transformations you've undertaken in your own life or helped others with. People will pay you to help them go from point A to point B. So, what's the point B you can help them reach?

- Who might need what you have to offer? (That's called your target demographic.) Research these people and figure out their pain points and goals. Then create an offering that helps them reach their goal while eliminating their pain points. For example, "We'll paint your walls in one day so you don't waste your weekend doing it!"

- For people with gifts like yours, what promotional platforms are already in place? If you're selling jewelry, it's Etsy. If you're looking to make money from your music, it's Spotify. It's easier to hitch yourself to a wagon that's already got momentum than to build your own platform from scratch. Go where the people already are. Remember my client Marina, the singer who went to Julliard? Her music is streaming on Spotify. That's a lot smarter than busking at the farmers market, hoping that a friendly shopper will drop a dollar into your red velvet hat.

- Who can you learn from so that you can build it right the first time? Who is building your type of business or side gig? Learn from them. (I offer courses on this, just sayin'.) Paying money up front for support saves you costly time and money mistakes down the road. Pretending you can do it all on your own is a great way to stay exactly where you are.

STEP 4: Convey your value to others.

Now that *you* have discovered your genius, how do you get *others* to see it? Let's talk about how you can articulate your gifts when you're talking to an employer, an interviewer, or a potential client. I'm going to teach you a nifty little acronym that turns your gifts into accomplishment statements. At the end of the day, people want to know that you can drive tangible outcomes. So take the GO-CAR for a spin.

> *GO-CAR: Gift + Opportunity + Context + Activity + Result =*
> *Accomplishment Statement*
>
> **[Gift]** One of my best gifts is _____.
>
> **[Opportunity]** An opportunity I had to harness this gift occurred when _____.
>
> **[Context]** I was working at _____ in the _____ role where I did _____.
>
> **[Activity]** The activity I did that showcased this gift was _____.
>
> **[Result]** As a result, _____ happened.

Here's an example from Rosie, an engineering grad:

[Gift] One of my best gifts is creative problem solving.

[Opportunity] An opportunity I had to harness this gift occurred last year when our engineering company was building a new development and several big trees needed to be removed. Initially, my boss wanted to take them to another site, yet it was hours away and the fuel for the trucks would have been expensive.

[Context] I was working at Acme Inc. as the engineering intern and I supported the project manager by doing cost estimates and evaluations.

[Activity] I brainstormed ways we would sell these logs and repurpose them. As a summer intern, I had some spare time on my hands so I wanted to take this project on myself. I asked my boss if I could and he said yes. I found a company that was within twenty minutes of the job site that bought our logs to repurpose them into sustainable wood tables. It was a win-win because they paid for the logs and our trucks could easily drop them off on their way back into town so there weren't any major excess fuel charges.

[Result] As a result, my boss was so impressed that I was handed the opportunity to work on an even bigger project that summer.

Conveying your value is about storytelling. (And no, you don't need to be Jane Austen penning *Pride and Prejudice* to be a great storyteller.) Telling your story is about making sure you hit all the letters of GO-CAR in an interview. That way you can fill the other person in on your past experiences in a clear, articulate way.

The key is to always back your gifts and genius up with proof and concrete examples. If you have numbers to back things up, even better.

("I increased sales by 20 percent." "I was able to grow my team from two to twenty." "I signed a client that was worth $150K.") If you don't have numbers, use big achievements. ("I won an award for my research." "I was invited to be on the board." "The queen asked me to lunch.")

STEP 5: Know when you are in the zone.

A big part of being in your genius is knowing when you are in it—and when you have a little farther to travel. That's okay. When you are trying a new way to express your genius, it might take some trial and error before you hit your stride. Don't give up.

Based on your gifts, you might try a more technical role at work and hate it. Or you might start a side gig and think, *Oh dang, this is not my thing.* You may need to experiment with a few things before you hit the nail on the head and think, *Ohhh, this is my genius! I love this!*

Only taking action will give you clarity on your true purpose.

For me, it's gone like this:

I could do tech start-ups! Oh, this is ending miserably . . .
I could invent a fiber cookie! This recipe is giving me a lot of gas.
I could write poetry! Oh my god, this is mortifying. I will die if
*   anyone sees this.*

Once I finally landed on business coaching, then I knew I was actually in the zone.

So don't give up if your first try fails, or even your second or third. It's all practice for where you're going, so don't sweat it.

Part 3

Ditch the Doubts That Hold You Back

Now that you've found your genius, let go of the doubts that hold you back from doing it.

chapter 16

"I Can't Do That. Other People Can, but Not Me."

When I was in business school, my friends and I used to sit down and talk about our big 'n' juicy goals for our lives. One quiet weekend, my pal and I plunked ourselves down in funky leather chairs at our local hipster coffee joint. You know, the kind where lattes are five bucks plus a dollar extra for almond milk they make in-house by hand-squeezing nuts through some sort of sack.

My friend said to me, "So, Kelly. If you could do anything with your life, what would that be?"

"Oh!" I said. "That's easy. I would be like Danielle LaPorte."

In case you've been living under a rock, Danielle LaPorte is an author, speaker, and writer who talks about spirituality, your desires, and living heart-centered. She lives in my city and is one of the coolest cats in town.

Because I grew up in a neighborhood populated by accountants, engineers, doctors, and lawyers, I didn't know many people making a living from something creative. Nobody around me had the kinds of jobs that required you to explain what you do for a living. ("So, uh, you're a life coach? What does that mean, exactly?") This was before Instagram, *The 4-Hour Workweek*, and the concept of lifestyle design, so I was completely in the dark. I didn't realize that doing something different was a possibility until I saw that Danielle actually had a website, and books, and *was making some serious million-dollar moolah.*

Deep in my heart, I knew what I always wanted to do with my life. I wanted to write books and speak on stages. At eighteen, "become Danielle LaPorte" was the best way I could describe what I wanted to do.

"Great! So how can you do that?" my friend asked.

I cut my friend off before he even finished speaking.

"Ohhh! I can't do that!"

That was the end of our conversation and I changed the subject because I could feel myself starting to blush. Getting embarrassed when you already have rosacea makes people go, "Whoa, are you okay? What's wrong with your face? It's, like, really red."

I used to believe that my dreams were better suited for other people. Special people. Talented people. You know, the kinds with great gifts and pure strokes of genius. So, not me. Other people could do big, courageous things with their lives, and I needed a corporate job because I wasn't "bold" like them. Other people could pursue their highest callings and I needed to "stick it out" in subpar work experiences because I wasn't as innovative as them. Other people could make a living by pursuing their art and creative work, but I needed to "do something serious with my life." I couldn't be just sitting around all day writing poetry. I needed to solve world hunger or something.

Once I found Danielle LaPorte, I found other life coaches, leadership teachers, and thought leaders. Yet the problem was that I thought these folks were light-years away from me and I put 'em on a pedestal. They were actually remarkable, whereas I was super-duper not. And they were genuinely cool. Which I definitely wasn't either. So I felt stupid for blurting this embarrassing fantasy out loud.

This is one of the biggest lies we tell ourselves: our deepest dreams are exclusively for other people and not us. We say, *Yeah, sure, other people can do that . . . but* not *me.*

She can do it because she's super smart . . . but not me.
He can start that because he's so bright . . . but I can't.
They can do that because they are actually skilled . . . but I'm not.

We talk ourselves out of job opportunities, career advancements, business endeavors, books we've always wanted to write, and songs we've always wanted to sing because we believe this lie.

When we buy into the lie that our dreams aren't meant for us, we deny our genius. If you pursued that relentless dream, you'd tap into your most sacred gifts. And I dunno . . . *stumble upon your purpose?*

If that's not motivating enough for you, let me inform you of this: your dreams were given to you for a reason. Yep, you. You were specifically chosen for the journey, and the universe thought you were so insanely awesome that it assigned *you* with this cool new endeavor. Therefore, when you assume you can't do it, it's like slapping the universe in the face when in fact it was the one who gave you the dream in the first place.

Lemme tell ya about Jody. She's a PhD student studying epigenetics and Parkinson's disease. She's one of the brightest people I know and we used to sit next to each other in AP biology. To me, Jody is the most gifted scientist I know, yet she had her doubts. She said,

"When I got into my PhD program and saw the other students, I felt like I wasn't smart enough. Others were so quick on their feet when answering questions from the professor. I can come up with a good answer, but I need to think about it first. In certain courses like statistics, it also took me longer to study the material and others were more naturally gifted at it. I was comparing myself to my peers and felt like maybe I wasn't completely suited for this. It's my biggest dream to keep studying ways to prevent disease, yet I considered quitting when I saw how sharp the others were. It took me a while, but I realized that this didn't make me a bad scientist. I just had different gifts around being logical, thinking big picture, and connecting the dots."

When it comes to your biggest dream, you're going to have your doubts. You'll compare yourself to others and feel as far away from greatness as Earth is from Pluto. But you can't let that stop you because, in a galaxy full of souls, you were chosen for the journey.

We all get very specific visions of what we should be doing with our life. For Jody, it was being a scientist. I know for me, deep down, I always knew that I wanted to be a teacher, speaker, and creator. When I tried to apply for marketing jobs, I'd get sidetracked by TED talks and think, *Gosh, it would be cool to be a speaker!* When I was building my start-ups, I'd listen to podcasts and think, *It would be so sweet if I had my own!* It was always the same shit over and over again. It was never the intuitive hit to become a pro golfer. Or an astronaut. Or even a real estate agent.

Your soul is silently pulling you in certain directions, so shut up for a second and listen. Because you just might be staring at your life's calling if you say yes.

chapter 17

"I'm Not Good Enough"

Were I to lie down on the couch of a therapist's office as she, sitting cross-legged with a pen and pad of paper, peered at me with her tortoiseshell glasses sliding down her nose while asking me what obstacles stand in the way of me becoming Danielle LaPorte, then I might have an answer for her.

If you could get to the core wound in my heart, it would be, "I'm not good enough."

Now, let me explain how this therapy session would have gone. To begin with, I would have used an entire box of tissues by the time she asked me that question (even though I'd have gone into the session telling myself I wouldn't cry because I had a meeting after this). And my mascara would be running down my face. And I'd have left feeling great, but also like I'd just hurled up a hair ball and gotten somethin' really nasty outta me. It's like that relief you feel after you vomit? Yeah, that.

If she had probed more and asked, "Kelly, why don't you feel good enough to do this work?" I could have rattled off a huge list:

- "Oh god, my writing sucks!"
- "My work is nowhere on the level of Danielle LaPorte's."
- "Have you seen how good her books are? I can't do that!"

One of the false doubts we face is that we're not good enough. Not good enough to start. To try. Or to even hand in the résumé. That we don't have enough experience. Or talent. And that, maybe worst of all, everything we've done so far is subpar. *I should have had better results. I should be farther along by now. I should be more accomplished. I should have more to show for myself.*

About two years ago, I read a self-help book in which the author said that you were "born worthy" and you don't have to do anything to "be worthy." I laughed and thought she was lying. In all honesty, I was consistently looking for my worth outside myself and comparing myself against others 24/7 to see how I stacked up. *Danielle's writing is great. Mine is garbage.* These comparisons only made me buy even more into the doubt that I wasn't good enough. I also believed that my worth came from my work. Which made me think that whatever the hell I did wasn't enough because others were always doin' it better. If I had four clients, I thought I should have five. Despite doing six-figures sales, I needed to push for seven. *Because, you know,* then *I'd actually be successful.*

Here's what you need to know: your genius is already inside you. You're naturally incredible at it, and you don't have to "try" to be great at it. You already are. You don't need anyone's approval, and you don't need someone to tell you that you are worthy. In fact, striving for external proof of your worth only pushes you farther down the rabbit hole of old-school success.

I wish I'd dropped this rickety doubt a long time ago. Looking back, I spent so much time worrying about my enoughness that I wish I had just shut up and done what I wanted already.

If you find yourself doubting your abilities, I have an exercise for you. Instead of questioning the crap out of yourself, try looking back to past examples of times when you experienced sweat-inducing levels of self-doubt, but you kept calm, carried on, and ended up kicking some major ass.

If my therapist had asked me *another* question, it might have been this: "Can you recall a time when you thought you weren't good enough? But in reality, you were?"

(For the record, why do they ask so many questions? Why can't they just give me a five-step action plan on a sticky note and let me leave forty-five minutes early? Then I wouldn't need to pay the receptionist with puffy eyes while snorting back snot.)

In response to this question, I would have told my therapist about the time I was in seventh grade going into eighth. In my neck of the woods, we had an elementary school that went from kindergarten to grade seven, and then you went straight to high school for the rest of the ordeal. This meant that when your cozy, happy elementary school days were up, you had to go to the big, scary school with teenagers. I remember crying on my last day of grade seven because of this. *Will bullies smash me against the locker? Will the lunch tables be as catty as they are in the movies?* I had all summer to agonize over this. *Am I ready? Am I good enough? Am I smart enough? I mean, the next step after this is . . . college.*

Do you wanna know how the first day of high school went? I don't even remember it. I was totally fine and I made it out alive. I think I actually had fun.

We waste a lot of time questioning our enoughness. Our competence. Our talent. And it's all a big waste of time. In the end, you'll be totally fine. Just like me on my first day of high school.

This is why I wish I'd given up the habit of doubting myself sooner. I could have had a fun summer before high school instead of spending those sunny days fretting. I could have started doing my genius earlier instead of lamenting over how lousy I was. And when it came to my coaching business, I could have launched sooner. I had the talent; I just had a truckload of fear standing in my way.

Despite having the right gifts, we doubt ourselves for months, years, and even decades. Who knows, maybe even for past lifetimes? But I wanna let you know that you're not alone. Do you remember Tera, the Olympic swimmer? The doubt of "I'm not good enough" was one that came up for her—big-time. In high school, her coaches knew it would be tough for Tera to make the Olympic team because she was up against so many other successful swimmers, so she joined the National Training Center where all the all-stars were doing laps. She improved by swimming alongside them and measuring her performance against theirs. Soon it was time to take a stab at scoring a spot on Team Canada for the London 2012 Olympics. It all came down to one event: qualifying at trials. Remember, Tera had been swimming for almost a decade at this point. She said, "I only truly believed that I was good enough to qualify for the Olympics one month before the Olympic Trials." People in the back, did you hear that? Even the most successful folks are doubting themselves all the way up until showtime. Yet they lean into their gifts, trust that everything they've done so far has been enough, and go for it.

Here's the aha moment I want you to have: When you know your genius, you know that you are enough. You have enough gifts. You have enough skill. When you know your red thread, you know you have enough experience. **The ego's favorite chant is the one of inadequacy. But your soul will always sing the truth of who you really are.**

If you have the courage to believe that you are a genius in a world that's telling you that you're not, then you'll finally realize that you are enough.

chapter 18

"I Need More Time, Experience, and Maybe Another Certification"

In the wee early days of my health blog, I thought it would be a good idea to write down everything I knew and sell it as an e-book. And I kid you not, I titled it *Fuck This Shit I'm Curing Myself: How to Ditch Chronic Illness and Get Yourself a Life*. We all need to have a moment of silence for how mortifying that title is, but I digress.

The goal of this cleverly titled e-book was to share stress-relieving tips, some mindset tools, and a plant-based recipe or two. But before I started writing, I had an internal freak-out: I wasn't a doctor, I never went to med school, and I wasn't even a nutritionist.

Naturally, I decided to start looking into med schools. *Being an MD would make me super legit, right? I mean, I hate science but I could stick it out just to get those two little letters. Or even a PhD. Gosh, that would be good enough.*

I literally Googled "how to get into med school" and other search terms like "easiest places to get into med school" and "offshore Caribbean med schools." I genuinely believed that if I wanted to write a little ol' book with some mantras and a nice vegan muffin recipe, I needed to be a freaking doctor. (And don't worry, I wasn't giving medical advice, so there was no need to be one.)

At this moment in my life, I had six years of experience managing my autoimmune condition daily. From understanding which foods would make me flare up to making the necessary lifestyle shifts, I knew this information like the back of my hand. From the lens of life experience, I was a pro. But on paper? Not exactly. So I decided that some fancy certifications would make me more legit.

Don't make this mistake in your own life.

If I'm being honest, this wasn't about going to med school for myself. It was to look good in the eyes of others since I worried about what they'd think.

I was sure that people would say:

"Who do you think you are?"
"Are you even qualified to do this?"
"You don't have enough experience."
"Who's ever going to listen to you?"

With my book, I was seriously concerned that people would say this to my face. Because, on the inside, this is what I was thinking and I was simply waiting for someone to admit it out loud.

When it comes to pursuing our most creative work at perhaps our most courageous moments, it's extremely tempting to think we need more.

We need more things on our résumé to prove to other people that we are qualified enough.
We need more accolades to illustrate that we are smart enough.
We need more sales under our belt to showcase that we are experienced enough.

We feel like we're only one degree away from feeling valuable and not having impostor syndrome.

In reality, your genius has been at play for years now. You've had decades to hone it and perhaps didn't even notice the knowledge you were accumulating. Yes, even in that summer job scooping ice cream and that extracurricular you did in college. Look, you can always get more time, experience, and a degree down the road. But my best advice for you is to try now anyway and see how it goes. You might be surprised.

Now, this is a tricky doubt to grapple with. Sometimes, yes, you do need a degree. Or an employer wants to see more years of experience on your résumé. Yet here's what I can tell you: You're smarter than you think. You've mastered your genius more than you know.

Look how it worked out for Kerri, the money coach you met in chapter four. She said:

I definitely felt not good enough at the start and thought I needed more qualifications and experience, specifically around financial planning models. I also doubted if I could actually help anyone. That anxiety manifested as procrastination and feeling overwhelmed. I overcame it by taking small steps, pushing myself enough to keep moving forward, and leaning into the mantra of "done is better than perfect." I planned tiny tasks and celebrated my accomplishments no matter how small. I knew I wanted to help people with their finances to create financial freedom. So I found that inner motivation and just took the leap. And my first client came! I didn't feel ready, but we started. My first client found value and success from our work together. And then another client came! And this person also benefitted from our work together. Little by little, my confidence was growing. And with each coaching session, I noticed how much I enjoyed it, how present I was, and that I was in my genius.

How does Kerri's story end? With her continuing to book paid clients and not going back to school. Even if you do want to go back to school, at some point you still need to start. So, why not try now? This strategy worked for Kerri.

Now Jena, the graphic designer you met in chapter two, felt like she had enough schooling, but not enough years of experience. She said:

> *I considered starting my own business for four years, prior to actually doing it. The entire year before I left my corporate job, I knew that I wanted to leave and start my own thing . . . but I was so nervous about actually doing it. I felt like I needed to prepare more, have twenty-plus freelance clients booked, and have tons of experience . . . all before leaving my job. I remember thinking to myself, "I'll be ready when . . ." and making an endless list of things I needed to "check off" to feel fully prepared.*

How does Jena's story end? By taking the plunge and outearning her corporate salary by the end of her first year in business. She did this because she stopped doubting her experience and started realizing how freaking great of a graphic designer she was already.

As in Kerri's and Jena's stories, diving in with two feet and finding some initial momentum can get you over the mindset trap of assuming you need more. Seeing the power your genius holds—in real situations!—can help you break up with the belief that you need more time, experience, and certifications.

Now, I'm gonna be real with you. This is an unconventional book. I mean, I promised you that from the beginning, so ya can't start complaining that you've been bamboozled now. I'm going to let you in on a secret, so if you're busy multitasking and simultaneously picking your nose as you read this book, focus for a sec. One reason I've gotten to where I wanna go so quickly is that I have no regard for the rules. (Rules!

Boring! Yawn. No, thanks.) Now, sometimes this gets me in trouble. But we're not going to focus on that because it mostly helps me get ahead.

Even though I'm quivering in my boots when I'm attempting something audacious, I try anyway and let experience be my teacher, not my fear. If I get rejected, fine. Then I go back to the drawing board and get more experience under my belt. But if it's smooth sailing, then I just did a huge power-up in what I thought was possible. And huzzah! I continue on my merry way.

When I began my entrepreneurial journey, I assumed there was going to be some sort of weird gatekeeper who'd stop me from going past certain limits. Moving to San Francisco, launching start-ups, applying for prestigious programs taught by billionaires, calling myself a coach, accepting real money for said coaching, and writing my first book with some colorful language in the title. A gatekeeper or naysayer would speak up, right? Nope. Nada. (Except the stupid reader who emailed me to say I listed "banana" *twice* in a bullet point list somewhere inside *Fuck This Shit I'm Curing Myself.* And rudely told me it was overpriced at $29 given this inexcusable typo.) Anyhoo . . . aside from her, nobody really stopped me. So I just kept going.

But before I was this nonconformist YOLO-er, I was a goody-two-shoes who played dutifully by the unsaid rules of society. I used to believe that I needed ten years of corporate experience before I started a business. I worried that twenty-two was too young to have a start-up in Silicon Valley. And don't you need an MBA to charge for business consulting? I thought I needed to climb ladders. And fit in with my peers. And get certifications like everyone else.

When you go against that, you become a maverick. You become a rule breaker. You become one of the brave. And last time I checked, seriously brave, self-taught masters who forged their own path are pretty cool. (That is, unless you don't think Richard Branson is cool. Then we need to talk . . .)

Confidence coupled with your genius can get you farther ahead in life than fear fused with endless degrees. So use the mantra "Try now." Try applying for the dream job now. Try starting your side hustle now. Try taking that leap of faith now.

Here's how to overcome your doubt and get started:

1. **Make a list of your greatest accomplishments.**

    Instead of having such a narrow focus on what you lack, acknowledge what you have. One way you can see this is to write a list of all the major things you've done in your life that you're proud of and stick it to your wall. And when you get frozen in fear, remember that you've *already* accomplished so much.

    Plus, the biggest moments of expansion follow the pattern of faith first, results second. So bonus points if you can find examples of when you had some seriously firm faith *first*, took action despite being scared shitless, and saw some rad results in return. Most folks have this backward. People usually think that getting results gives you the faith to take action. Not the case, young grasshopper. Faith comes first, then results follow suit. No amount of time, experience, and education will ever give you complete certainty.

2. **Ask inverse questions when you assume "If I had X, then I'd get Y."**

    Challenge your thoughts with the contrary: in my coaching practice, I call this "inverse thinking," where I reframe the question back to you so you can take a more empowering view. Here are some examples:

    Thought: *If I get into grad school, then they will take me more seriously.*

Inverse Question: What if you take yourself more seriously? If you were as confident as the top person on your team, do you think you'd really need more schooling? Is it a lack of schooling you have . . . or a lack of confidence?

Thought: *If I get certified in this healing modality, then it will attract more clients.*

Inverse Question: Will it? Or do you just feel inadequate about your own genius? This is some tough love, but in business it's not the most educated person who wins. It's the person who puts themselves out there and gets pretty damn good at the scariest part: sales.

Thought: *If I had a major company on my résumé like everyone else who is applying, then I'd stand out more to employers.*

Inverse Question: What if you leveraged what you already had? And if everyone else who's applying has similar experience at major companies, don't you think you might stand out even *more* by being different?

3. **Take the flipped perspective to remove the constraints of time, experience, and education.**

    This is a mindset strategy that I came up with when I was trekking solo through Italy when I was twenty years old. I was terrified. This was my first time traveling alone, which meant I needed to strike up convos with strangers, say *scusi*, and confirm that I was on the right side of the train platform. Meaning, I couldn't beg a bolder friend or parent to do it on my behalf. Every time I felt scared, I told myself I had to flip the thought around and do it anyway.

I coined the phrase "taking the flipped perspective" to describe this concept.

Here's how you harness it:

- If you think you need ten years of experience under your belt to launch a business, how can you launch before the end of the month?
- If you've had your eye on an internship forever but have always been too nervous to apply, what if you had to submit an application by Sunday?
- If you're scared to ask the hot Italian man in fine, beige linen pants beside you for directions, how can you do it now in the next five seconds?

When we flip the script, it invites possibility and, most importantly, tells our fear to take a hike. Having a deadline forces you to drown out the doubt.

You don't need more time. You just need to get going. You are *already* excellent at your genius. Don't let thinking you need another degree or certification hold you back. Those doubts are simply your inner critic's safety blanket. Instead of falling prey to this stall tactic, give yourself permission to go for it now.

Take the flipped perspective and begin today, instead of attempting to score more time, experience, and maybe a certification. (Or two if you're really scared.) Plus, sometimes taking a certain opportunity or adding another degree is our ego's way of delaying starting because we think we need more accolades under our belt in order to begin, worry we're not good enough, or are simply too scared to say yes to our calling.

You're ready when you say you are.
And you're ready right now.

Things to remember when you are Googling "offshore med schools in the Caribbean":

- You'll never feel ready to start. The "readiness" comes from the experience of doing the thing in real time. It's ironic, but it's true.

- When you say, "I need more time. I can't start now; I'm not ready!" be real with yourself. Is this the truth or are you just scared to start?

- People always want to learn from those who've been in their shoes and who are one step ahead of them. (That's why we search "how to fix the drain" on YouTube and watch how someone else did it.) So don't trick yourself into thinking that your past experience isn't good enough. If you've created a positive outcome for yourself or someone else, then that makes you qualified to help. Yep, that's it. (Unless this is a regulated industry, cuz you can't say "screw you!" and start a dentistry practice in your living room.)

- Whenever you're debating signing up for something, ask yourself: *Am I doing this because I don't feel good enough? Or am I doing this because I feel called to do it, regardless of the piece of paper I'll get at the end?*

- Take the flipped perspective. What if you *don't* need more time, experience, or another certification? What if you could do it right now?

chapter 19

"I Need to Move to Bali"

About once a year, I get this urge to move to Bali. It comes every fall as the clouds begin to settle in Vancouver, right about when I start hating my life and resenting the fact that I live in a rain forest where it pours 165 days a year.

Three things always come to mind:

1. Buy a new navy-blue coat. Specifically, one that I've been trying to track down since I saw a fashion blogger wearing it three years ago and it's no longer in stock. (AKA retail therapy.)

2. Get a radical new haircut. (*Cut it all off? Dye it blonde? Shall I try bangs? Because, you know, a new haircut will make me feel like a new person. My life will suddenly get way cooler and awesome.*)

3. Move. Either to California or Australia or Hawaii or Bali. (Then I get overwhelmed with how I'll move, worry that the airline will break my beloved iMac, and decide that buying the navy coat and living here is the better, easier option.)

I personally blame Julia Roberts in *Eat Pray Love* for this annual yearning. Because eating all that pizza in Naples and having all that sex in Bali with Javier Bardem looks way more fun than whatever the hell I'm doing right now. I hate to admit it, but as I write this book in the middle of fall, I've already fantasized over all three. Instead of actually finishing my book, I've started a new Pinterest board called "Haircut Inspo," debated if Santa Barbara or Santa Monica is a better place to live, and pulled out the credit card to buy a new navy coat. Because if I had these three things, *then* it would make writing *wayyy* easier.

One of the lies we tell ourselves is that we need different circumstances before we start.

We say things like:

> *I need to book a babysitter for my kids and* then *I'll start.*
> *I need a new office nook with the right ergonomic chair and* then *I'll start.*
> *I need a day to myself, alone in the house, to do my best thinking and* then *I'll start.*

You don't need to move to Bali and *Eat Pray Love* your life to create a new, radical expression of genius. You can just do more of what you're already good at. If your tax accounting job lights you up because it feels like solving a complicated puzzle every day when you sit down at your desk, then keep doing it. But don't make the mistake of thinking you need a trust fund and two years abroad with limited Wi-Fi service to create a unique expression of your soul. Don't assume that you need a five-hour Transcendental Meditation practice to "get in the flow" and the latest laptop to produce your best work. Your genius doesn't need all those fancy bells and whistles. It just wants you to spend time with it.

You will always be lured by the new IKEA catalog to spruce up your office or be tempted by warmer climates to quit your life and move. So don't believe the lie that *if* you had a better environment, *then* you'd start doing your genius.

Things to remember when you're trying to track down that sold-out navy coat on eBay . . . even though you'll never find it:

- The more frustrating your current circumstances, the more alluring the fantasy of a new environment is. But running away from your life doesn't work. I've tried it before. When you hit this feeling, ask yourself: *What am I trying to run away from or avoid?* Sometimes, it's the hard conversation, the hard choice, or the hard thing in front of you. (Like writing the effing book.)

- One of the games I like to play with myself is to take away little things that my ego holds on to so that I remember that my genius will always flourish regardless of conditions. (*Oh, you want to fly to Palm Springs and write this book in peace? How about you write this at your parents' house where they still have a landline phone that rings every five minutes?*)

- The beauty of being a master is that you can make use of whatever you have on hand to create your masterpiece. I mean, Pablo Picasso drew masterpieces on the back of a napkin. It's your ego that tricks you into thinking you need a huge-ass canvas and a room dedicated as your art studio.

- Get in the habit of not making excuses. (*I don't have the money, the time, the experience, the right lamp . . . Blah blah blah.*) Take note of what you *do* have.

- People who stay stuck are the ones who think their external reality dictates their internal one. It's actually the reverse. For years, I felt stuck because I was living at my parents' house, or in the wrong relationships, or working at a job I didn't like. In fact, "feeling stuck" was probably the most overused phrase in my journal. And if anyone read it, they'd think, *Has this girl ever seen a thesaurus?* I thought that my external circumstances held me back internally from going for what I most wanted in life. But when you change the inside (aka your thoughts, beliefs, and actions), the outside ends up changing. Usually, exactly how you want it to.

chapter 20

"Someone Is Already Doing It,
So I Can't"

I found a rusty old journal from a few years ago. Sometimes, I'm nervous to crack open my old journals out of fear of what I'll find, but I almost always get a good laugh. Like this back-to-back entry from the same week of university.

> **Date:** Monday, November 3, 2014
> **Title:** Things I Love About My Life!
> **CliffsNotes Summary:** Talking about how much I love the guy I'm dating, my internship is going well, and school is good.

> **Date:** Tuesday, November 4, 2014
> **Title:** List of Things I FUCKING Hate.
> **CliffsNotes Summary:** Talking about how much I despise the guy I'm dating, my group project team member is a "dumb twit," and the accountant at my internship needs to stop chewing her gum so loud at her desk. I use lots of strong language like

"bunch of losers" and insist that everyone around me should "stop being so f*cking stupid."

This sounds a lot like Katy Perry's pop hit "Hot N Cold."

Now that I think of it, "hot 'n' cold" sounds like my former self whenever I thought of something new.

For a second, I'd think I was the smartest person in the world with the coolest idea ever. I'd jump with joy, call my mother as if I just won the lottery, and burst with possibility. *I could totally sell this! And then Oprah will call! And maybe Reese Witherspoon will share it on her Instagram! Actually, scratch that—she'll love it so much that she'll message me and we'll become BFFs!* Then, two minutes later, after I Googled it, I'd feel defeated when I saw that it already existed.

New ideas and plans for my life always went like this.

I'd think of an awesome business concept, but then find out someone else was already doing it and doing it far better than me—to the tune of $12 million a year in sales. Plus, she was wickedly well-connected. She even had photos of herself with Tony Robbins, Oprah, and the freaking pope on her website. *The pope? Are you kidding me? I can't compete with this!*

I'd want to launch a podcast and then stumble upon some rock star who was already knee-deep in 154 episodes, had two million downloads, and had already interviewed both GaryVee and Glennon Doyle. *Well, I'm screwed.*

I'd think of a cookbook to create and someone would say to me, "Oh, have you read the *Oh She Glows* cookbook?" Then I'd check it out at the bookstore and realize that there was no longer any need for my plant-based cookbook.

Seeing other people already doing what I wanted to do was extremely frustrating.

One of the lies we tell ourselves is, "Someone is already doing it, so I can't." We fear that our ideas are already taken, that our dreams have been done before, and that because someone else is successfully doing what we intended to do, we can't pursue it too.

The good news is that you don't need to worry about this. Here are four reasons why.

Reason 1: When you honor your genius, you'll recognize that you are in competition with no one.

You are the differentiating factor, no matter how many times something has been done before. Even if there are millions of other blogs or competing job applicants, nobody has the exact same blend of lived experiences as you. Nobody has seen life through your eyes, endured your traumas, and had the same heartbreaking setbacks. Nobody thinks the same way or has the same vision or wisdom. Because of all that, you create *your* way of doing things.

You are the competitive advantage. Because, at the end of the day, people are buying or hiring *you*. Your heart. Your intellect. Your genius. So it's wrong to assume that if someone else is already doing something similar, then you can't. Because they are not you. No two souls are alike, and even twins don't have the same fingerprints.

Reason 2: Don't see competition as a red light. See it as a green one.

Imagine if Steve Jobs had said, "Well, the CD Walkman has already been made, so who would really need an iPod? I mean, everyone in their '90s tracksuits already looks like they are getting their musical needs met as they jog around the block, so I guess I'll just give up, put my hands in my pockets, and sulk as I walk home with my head down."

That would be ridiculous, right?

Swap your thinking from scarcity to abundance and realize that if someone is doing what you want to do, that means they could be a role model for you, there's already an established market, and it must be lucrative if people are buying it. Competitors are a sign that you're on the right path. Don't feel bummed. Instead, congratulate yourself on having great ideas.

Plus, if your concept already exists, you'll have an easier time setting up shop because customers already understand it. For example, if you wanna open a coffee shop, everyone already knows how great a cup of joe is, which means you don't need to educate people about the benefits of coffee. It's actually harder to sell something new because you need to spend a lot of marketing dollars just to teach people what it is and why it's great. Competition is good because your competitors have paved the way to make your product or service mainstream. You just need to put your spin on it, add your genius, and boom! Your organic coffee shop with Instagramable cute pink walls is now open for business.

Reason 3: There will always be customers who want something different from what's currently being offered.

Even if there are a bunch of industry leaders or a competitor has a strong hold on the market, there's always going to be the customer who wants something a little different. It's just about niching down and knowing what *you* can uniquely bring to the table. It's your genius and hot take on the situation.

Truth be told, I've never understood the fuss about mayo. It's flavorless and weird. And what's the deal with the raw eggs? One day, I bought vegan chipotle mayo because I was in a rush and needed a dipping sauce for my yam fries. I was taking them to a party and thought, *People like mayo, right? This will work.* Anyway, I tried it. Now I can't get enough of the stuff.

The mayonnaise industry is a $13.5-billion-dollar one. And if you were trying to get into it, you might think that the competition is stiff and there's no room for you. You might say that it's been done before, every kitchen already has a jar somewhere in the back of the fridge, and you're outta luck. No matter how many brands are on the market, there could be a Canadian gal standing in Whole Foods in a rush on a Friday night who would totally buy something a little different if it was there. That's where *your* vegan chipotle mayo comes in.

Somebody wants what you've got, even if you keep discrediting it or don't think it's that special.

How is this all applicable in your life?

Instead of lamenting over how many other real estate agents there are in your city and then using it as fuel for your case *against* your genius, remember that you can offer something different in a crowded field. No matter how good Sally's real estate ad looks at the bus stop, some people might wanna hire you because you grew up in the neighborhood. So don't make the mistake of assuming that there's no room for you. Because there is.

Here are a few ways to find your version of the "vegan chipotle mayo" in your life.

If you're a student trying to get into college, tell admissions what makes *you* unique and don't be shy about it. My business school application was a creative essay about my love for making jewelry. Specifically, "the possibility of something beautiful, not yet given form."

(Very poetic, thank you.) It was certainly a risk; it was artsy and heavy on the metaphors. But I weaved it in with my goal of becoming an entrepreneur. How many other kids wrote an application based on the metaphor of jewelry making? Probably zero. The majority likely droned on about grades and other generic stuff that admissions has seen a zillion times. Anyhoo, they gave me the thumbs-up and I got into a school with a 6 percent acceptance rate. My point? Leverage what makes you different.

If you're on a team vying for a promotion, articulate what *you* can do that nobody else can and back it up with proof from the past. Remember Joanna, who wanted that product manager role at Uber but lacked the technical background? She relied on the fact that she oversaw operations for countless global cities in her current role. Sure, others can code, but how many applicants can say they have experience like that? Find that one thing you have that nobody else in the stack of résumés does and talk about it.

If you're changing careers, use your outside knowledge to your advantage. If everyone's a longtime accountant and you're picking up accounting after being a professional baker, explain how your genius transfers and leverages your ability to see things with fresh eyes. That outside perspective is more alluring to employers than you realize. Plus, when you're brand-new to something, having a beginner's mindset is actually an asset because you don't see the same obstacles as those who've been in the industry for a while. So play it up, buttercup.

Reason 4: Somebody is waiting for *your* way.

The world needs your genius and there is someone out there who wants to hear it in the way *you* say it. They are patiently waiting for the way *you* do it. There are clients, employers, and customers waiting for you. You might not see them on day one, but they are out there. Rumi said, "What you seek is seeking you," so if you want to create an ad agency where you help nonprofits, there is someone out there literally scouring the internet searching for "ad agencies for nonprofits." Your people exist. They are simply waiting for you to step into your genius and show up already.

chapter 21

"I Can't Make Money Doing That"

In university, I had a big ol' argument with my mother about my major. She insisted I do something "useful" with my business school degree and major in finance or accounting. A part of me agreed. Although in my heart I wanted to do marketing, I thought that would be "too easy" and I should use my degree to become a more well-rounded citizen of the world who was fluent in the language of stock tickers. Finance sounded very sexy and I could intern at Goldman Sachs like my peers, but I passed on it because majoring in finance was too boring. I also wasn't a good fit anyway. Turns out, they won't hire you just because you want to go to New York and wear kitten heels that clack on the lobby's marble floor. That left accounting, which was not good since I'd only scored 64 percent in my first class. It was hard. I barely understood it. (I still barely understand it.)

Given the level of difficulty, I thought majoring in accounting would be a noble pursuit. It's the classic hero's story, right? I'd be like Rocky

Balboa summiting the steps, but instead I'd be crunching numbers in the silent section of the library. Anyway, I spent that whole year telling everyone that I was choosing accounting as my major over marketing.

Why?

Because I didn't think I could earn a living doing what I adored. I listened to social norms instead of my own heart. I went for what made sense on paper versus what I felt in my gut. And I told myself that marketing was fluffy and not serious enough. I talked myself out of doing what I wanted most.

There is an undeniable sting that comes with convincing yourself *out* of your desires. It's the kind of pain that leaves you with a heavy heart, and yet we do it all the time. We rationalize, justify, and convince ourselves that it's the right choice. This is all especially true when it comes to career and cash.

One of the biggest lies I told myself was that "I can't make money doing what I love." What I loved was easy. What I hated was hard. So, in my head, making money = doing what was difficult.

Money and struggle have been paired together for far too long, even though that combo sucks. It's like the fitness instructor who makes you do jumping jacks and burpees to warm up. *What, you want us to, like, die or something?*

Somehow, it's really respectable to sacrifice and slave away making money doing shit you hate. If you want a really boring, boo-hoo life, then, by all means, keep following that pattern to make a paycheck. A lot of people do. If you believe that you have to bust your ass in order to make a lotta dough, then you'll never allow yourself to do what you are good at. And getting paid for your genius will feel out of the question.

Never cashing in on what comes most naturally to you occurs for two reasons.

Reason 1: You don't value your gifts and genius.

You brush off your genius, don't believe it's important, and barely trust your innate talent. You say things like, "Oh, that's just a hobby," "This? It's just something I do on the side," or "Nah, I don't think I could ever charge for it." At the end of the day, you don't respect your gifts or see how awesome they are, so you go back to hard work for validation. People with high self-worth recognize their value. In turn, they charge for their talents and ask for what they deserve.

You see, self-worth and money go hand in hand. They are like two best friends. If you want to invite money to the party, then you gotta make sure you invite self-worth too. Otherwise, money ain't gonna show up on your doorstep with a case of coconut La Croix and a party hat on.

Here are a few ways to increase your self-worth:

- Saying no.
- Not settling for less than you deserve.
- Going for what you want versus what you think you can get.
- Having boundaries.
- Knowing when it's time to walk away and doing so.
- Charging what you're worth. (Ahem, no discounts.)
- Letting go of the things that don't serve you.
- Not taking any shit.
- Valuing yourself enough to prioritize your own needs.
- Proudly proclaiming your gifts in a world where it's uncool to do that.
- Promoting yourself. And often.
- Trusting your gifts, rather than your inner critic and other dumbasses.

Your goal is to know that your genius has worth and you are deserving of what you desire. Which means doing that list above when the annoying requests and subpar offers come knocking. The next time you have an opportunity to step into your worth, do it. And bit by bit you will become a master.

Let me articulate how this works regarding getting paid for your genius:

- **Not settling.** "I'm desperate for this job, so I'll accept the salary they give me" versus "Let me negotiate for ten grand more because that's what my qualifications are worth in this industry."

- **Having boundaries.** "I'll give my Reiki healing away for free" versus "I'm charging $100 for this service at which I'm highly skilled."

- **Saying no.** "Sure, I'll give you advice pro bono and you can pick my brain for an hour" versus "I actually teach that in my course. I'll send you the link to the purchase page."

- **Listening to your inner critic.** "This painting I made is pretty, but I don't think anyone will buy it" versus "Let me make a website and see if I can sell this painting I'm proud of."

- **Not taking any shit.** "I'll just bill you at my freelance rate of $20 an hour if that's what you like" versus "I only work in defined packages. My starting rate is $5,000."

The more you swat away these subpar requests like a flyswatter slapping at a mosquito, the better you will feel and the more you'll say, "You know what? I am awesome. I do deserve better!" It's very similar to dating and relationships. After you've stepped into your worth, you might look back at your college boyfriend and think, *You are right! He* was *a total piece of trash!*

Lastly, self-worth is like a muscle. So, before you waltz into your boss's office and tell 'em that you want to move to the London office and get a $50,000 raise, start with the small stuff. Like telling the cashier they incorrectly charged you the full price for sweet potatoes that were on sale. (Nicely, of course.)

Reason 2: You don't think it's possible for you.

The second reason you might be saying "I can't make money doing that" comes from thinking success isn't possible for you.

There's a great story about the dude who ran the first four-minute mile. It used to be impossible; nobody could do it. But, one day, someone did. Two months later, two more dudes did it too. And now over a thousand runners have done it. Once somebody paves the way, the impossible feels probable. Something similar happens when it comes to you making money: if you have no examples of people who are monetizing their genius (aka nobody showing you that you can run a four-minute mile), then you'll never realize what you can also achieve.

The key trick here is to find relatable role models to show your subconscious mind. In the early days of my business, I found a few life coaches who had backgrounds similar to mine. Of course, Danielle LaPorte was the golden benchmark, but I still felt miles away from her best-seller success. Yet I found a life coach online who sold a $100 coaching package, also went to school for marketing (I picked marketing in the end, BTW), and worked at Lululemon for a while. Now, that I could totally relate to. And seeing her grow her business made it feel possible for me too. This is because of the subconscious mind.

Now, you've probably read other crunchy-granola books that talk about the subconscious mind. You know, the kinds where the authors wear only Birkenstocks and buy fluoride-free toothpaste. Well, it applies here. As a little psychology refresher, the subconscious mind is the part that does things on autopilot and stores information about things you do all the time—like driving a car or brushing your teeth with said toothpaste. The trick is to get your subconscious mind to believe that you can make money doing your genius. Your subconscious is kinda like a file cabinet. If it holds no records of people who ran the four-minute mile, then you'll have a hard time believing that it's possible. But what if you had a thousand files outlining all the athletes that ran it? Now your mind sees it as a possibility because you have so many examples of success.

Think of your journey to getting paid for your gifts as a file cabinet. Every time you see another human getting paid to do what you wanna do, add another file to the cabinet. At the start, you'll be skeptical. You have no proof that it's possible and you're all crotchety about the whole "make money doing what you love" concept. With more examples, the contents of the cabinet grow. And once the drawers are completely stuffed with articles and newspaper clippings of others succeeding, the subconscious mind believes that it's entirely feasible for you too.

You wanna build up your file cabinet, so your homework is to find five people who are doing exactly what you want to do in the world and study them until you know their journey inside out. The key thing here is that you need to see yourself in their shoes and story. They need to be *realistic* role models. Don't pick people who are a thousand steps ahead of you. Find the folks who are maybe only three to five steps ahead—like the life coach with the $100 coaching package rather than the author with one hundred thousand copies sold. It also helps when you can see yourself in their story. Perhaps you had similar upbringings, previously worked for the same company, or are both blue-eyed Geminis who have a habit of dating bad boys with tattoos. The goal is to look for specifics because you'll relate to your role model more. At the end of the day, you want your subconscious mind to latch on and think, *Oh! If this person can do it, then maybe I can too.*

Where do you find these people? Through the rabbit hole of the internet. YouTube channels, websites, podcasts, and social media are good places to start. These people don't need to be in your neighborhood or even live in your state. If you look hard enough, you will find that one random person in Utah who is selling organic wool macramé and making a small fortune on Etsy. Instead of feeling jealous, see them as your realistic role model.

In case you're scanning the horizon for some new role models, let me introduce you to a few. Since doubt about money is one of the biggest, hairiest beasts in the jungle, I wanna share how it surfaced for others. (Because you're in good company!) It's very easy to look at successful folks and think they're way better than you somehow. So I asked five clients, all people you've met in earlier chapters, to share how this doubt came up in their life *right* before they slapped a price tag on their genius and started takin' people's credit cards for it.

Let's talk about Marina, the singer. She earns royalties from her own tunes and charges hundreds for custom songwriting and music production. Marina said:

> So many people told me that "you can't make money doing music."
> I think we're conditioned as a society to believe that unless you're
> doing a set of certain professions, you won't make a good living, be
> seen as successful, or be taken seriously in your career. That mentality
> shaped my beliefs for so long, but my love for music never went away.
> I was so stubborn that I had to make it work.

Remember Nishi? She's the intuition coach and author who started helping others after her own struggles with anxiety. The one who scores $1,000 clients and quit her nine-to-five? Nishi said:

> Feeling unworthy kept me back. It played out as thoughts like "there
> are better coaches out there than me" and "people will never ever pay

me *money for anything." After a breaking point, I realized this was a self-imposed limit.*

Kristy, the life coach who now outearns her corporate salary, also had this doubt. Here's what she said about the early days:

Charging money for my gifts was hard. I felt like, "Who am I to start charging for this?" I had a feeling I'd be good at life coaching and others had established coaching businesses. But I thought . . . could I do it? Maybe I needed to work with people for free instead? It was really vulnerable to step into my genius and charge for it.

Do you remember Regena? The leadership coach and mindfulness teacher who scored a paid speaking gig at Google only one month after launching her business? And who now leads workshops everywhere else fancy-schmancy? Here's what she said:

I knew deep down that I was valuable and I had great ideas . . . but I worried that I wasn't good enough. Starting out from scratch was terrifying. I worried, "Am I doing this right? Did I give my clients enough value? Do I know what I'm talking about in this workshop?" I got so caught up in comparing myself to others and my mental dialogue was pretty much, "Look at how well so-and-so is doing it and how much they are charging. If I only had their presence or personality or hair." It took embracing self-compassion and recognizing my impact to realize that I was good enough to get paid for my genius.

Lastly, here's how this doubt surfaced for Jena. She was the graphic designer who handed in her nine-to-five resignation letter within six weeks of launching her business to go full-time on her own. She said:

I knew I wanted to leave my corporate job and make at least what I was earning on my own. But I had major doubts that I could achieve that. As a creative, I heard negative money stories about "designers" and "artists" not making a ton of money. Especially on their own as freelancers. This fear prevented me from believing in myself. I wasn't confident I could charge $2,500 for anything . . . plus I didn't know how to find anyone who would pay that.

(FYI, that $2,500 design package she was so nervous to sell—it's $7,500 now because she's that popular and talented.)

You ain't the only one, pal. Many have been where you are right now, so it's your job to go out there and find five realistic role models who expand your subconscious mind.

Things to remember when you're telling everyone that you'll be majoring in accounting even though you have no effing clue what the prof is saying:

- You can totally cash in on what comes most naturally to you. Getting paid for your genius comes down to two things: knowing your worth and proving to your subconscious mind that it's possible for you.

- To become iconic, you have to love what you do. Otherwise, when the shit hits the fan on the journey (and believe me, it will), the temptation to quit becomes hard to resist. So you have to follow the work that lights a flame in your heart. The craziest thing is that your genius is what you're most gifted at *and* what you love doing. If you're busy looking in the wrong direction in life (like me wanting to do accounting), you'll miss it.

- Money is a by-product of you living your genius. Everyone whose success you admire is harnessing their top three to five gifts all at once in their line of work. You'll be hard-pressed to find someone who isn't. Doing your genius is the only way to become truly exceptional.

chapter 22

"They'll Think Less of Me If I Go for It"

When I moved to San Francisco after business school, the biggest fear to rear its ugly head was, "They'll think less of me if I go for it." Because I was doing something different from my peers, I thought that people would question me in a "Who the hell do you think you are?" kinda way. So, as the confrontation-avoiding person that I am, I just didn't tell anyone what I was doing. As I sat at the airport waiting to board my flight, I thought, *Gee, I guess I should tell people now.* Then, naturally, I wondered, *What should I post on Facebook to announce the news?*

I wrote this whole post about how I'd turned down my job offers and uprooted my life. It was like ten paragraphs of that rah-rah, yada-yada, "follow your dreams" crap. Because I was so proud of myself for going for it, and thus wanted the whole world to know, I became an oversharer on social media. Looking back, to my horror, I realize I was "one of those people" who don't know when to shut the hell up and follow the unsaid rule of only *one* post per freakin' day. I droned on and on about my move, my start-ups, and everything cool 'n' swanky I was doing. My whole feed was like a shrine to San Francisco. I uploaded pics of the cable cars, crazy steep hills, and Victorian homes. I posted selfies with the Golden Gate Bridge, Alcatraz, and anything else that screamed "Toto, we're not in Canada anymore!"

The irony was that I'd run into people I knew all the time in San Francisco.

They'd say, "Hey, Kelly, what are you doing down here? Are you on vacation? Did you get a job here?"

And I would look at them and think, *Uh, I moved here. Did you not read my post?* I was slightly offended. My decision to move was, like, the news of the century. *I got a lotta likes on that post! Didn't everybody see that damn thing?* I really thought they had seen it. Yet this conversation was one that came up almost weekly.

"Yo, KT, what are you doing? Are you on vacation?"

I'd be like, "No . . . I'm working on my tech start-up."

And again.

"Oh, hey, KTrach! Are you applying for jobs here or something? Where are you staying? What hotel?"

"No! I'm living here. I'm working on my tech start-up."

It didn't end.

"Kel! Long time no see! Whatcha . . . ?"

"No! I'm *living* here!"

For fuck's sake! I moved *here. Tech start-up. Didn't you hear?!*

Up until this point in my life, I assumed that people were following my journey and keeping tabs on my career. I was sure people were curious about where I was working (was it impressive?) and what work I was doing (was it prestigious?).

I genuinely believed that people were clicking on my LinkedIn account 24/7 to see which logos peppered my profile, so I kept it in tip-top shape. Surely, recruiters were scrolling through my social media because I was top talent. (So there were no photos of me at frat parties. Not that I got invited to any.) And even ex-boyfriends were creepin' my Facebook page to see how accomplished I became after we broke up. Of course, they thought I was "the one who got away."

Maybe because business school is ultra-competitive and everyone is always trying to size up the competition or because we live in a world where social media makes us feel like we're the sun and everybody else revolves around us, I concluded that people deeply cared about what I was doing. Only in San Francisco did I realize that nobody was paying attention.

This realization was groundbreaking. (It was almost as groundbreaking as when I learned that pickles didn't come from a "pickle farm." They're just cucumbers.)

Yet I was always a wee bit conflicted. On the one hand, I felt badass about my start-ups. On the other hand, I thought that people would think less of me for doing this. As a former people pleaser, I wanted everyone to like me. But there were three people in particular who were of utmost importance to the health of my ego. They weren't super important folks in my life by any means. Yet my mind obsessed over what they would do/think/say if they found out. This list included a former roommate who I was always trying to impress (because I had a huge crush on him), my favorite boss (who I was hoping would hire me again in the future), and a former professor who I looked up to (but could never really tell if I had *finally* won him over or not). When I moved to San Francisco, I was deeply concerned about what they would think.

Well, Julian, Melissa, and Mr. Graham never said a peep. In fact, I don't even think they noticed.

Here's the aha moment I want you to have: **If you wanna be free, stop being dragged by other people's opinions.**

Here are five things I've learned over the years:

1. **Most people aren't going to give a crap about what you're doing with your life.**

   If you think random peeps care deeply about what you're doing, save yourself $2,000 a month on Bay Area rent (of a single room in a shared house) and take it from me: they don't. Everyone is concentrating on themselves and focusing on other things like handing in their presentation on time and secretly picking their wedgie at work. Nobody is really watching you too closely, so you might as well just do what you want.

2. **You can live your destiny or you can live in your head.**

   One of the reasons I didn't go for what I wanted sooner was because I was fixated on three people's opinions. *What would they say? Would they still respect me? Would they shake their heads disapprovingly?* I even went as far as to craft sentences that I'd say if I ran into them in person. (Especially Julian, for obvious reasons. And I'd better be lookin' cute as hell when I did.) You can spend your whole life being hooked on other people's opinions if you're not careful. Look, do you wanna impress people or fulfill your fate? Do you want to earn a Harvard degree to make your ma proud or to be on your own leading edge? Do you always want to be a mediocre fish in the sea because you're stagnated by what your boss thinks, or do you wanna give 'em the middle finger and go for it? You can forever clutch your fears like a grandmother grasps her pearls, or you can cut them loose and go for what you really want in life. The choice is yours.

   My client Kristy, the interior-designer-turned-life-coach, also faced the fear of judgment and here's how she overcame it. She said:

I was worried about what people would think because I was going into a different industry than I was previously in. Maybe they'd look at me and think, "Who does she think she is to give people advice on how to live their life?" Transitioning into the personal development world, I was concerned that my colleagues in my last industry would think it was too fluffy. What helped me shift through this fear was focusing more on the impact I wanted to make and the clients I wanted to help . . . instead of obsessing over what random people were thinking. The more I heard "Wow, this really resonates with me" from my target demographic, the more I felt motivated to continue sharing my message.

3. **Doing the unconventional increases the volume of your doubt.**

    My job offers after business school included a sales role and a marketing one—basically, two "normal" occupations for a recent grad. I did not make a huge deal in my head about these. But when I wanted to pivot to entrepreneurship? It was like all my fear, doubt, and worry held their largest press conference ever in my head. They all got gussied up in their crispest suits and yabbered on for hours makin' their cases. Sometimes, your highest form of genius and the work you really wanna do are creative. Maybe it's not what you went to school for and perhaps is just a hobby right now. These qualms can make things feel even *worse*. Doing the unconventional always comes with its doubts. You're not facing these doubts because you're weak; you're having them because you're on the verge of leveling up.

4. **Judgment usually comes from folks who've done far less than you.**

    Ninety-nine percent of people won't care what you do. But one teensy-weensy percent will. Unfortunately for you, they will also be the peskiest. I generally find that if you do get push-back, it comes from small minds who never once sought to start a side hustle with all the tips they saved up from waiting tables or moved across the country in a U-Haul. These folks denied their genius, abandoned their dreams, and settled for the status quo. Don't listen to 'em. Big minds don't criticize you, but small minds do. People who've done bolder things than you know what it's like to save those tips and make the leap. In turn, they'll show up for you with a big foam finger and cheer you on. It's the small minds that sneer and snicker.

5. **Feedback only counts when it's coming from the right source.**

Because small minds like to make snarky comments and scoff at your work, the dilemma is, Do you listen to the feedback or not?

I want you to visualize that you're a car in the middle of a busy highway. There are cars ahead of you and cars behind you. If we rank people on how much they are going after their aspirations, playing big with their life, and showing up wholeheartedly in their genius, there will always be people "ahead" of you who are rocking it. And there will be people "behind" you who *totally aren't.*

Say it's dark and your car headlights burn out. How do you know where to drive? That's easy—you follow the road by watching the red taillights from the dude ahead of you. The same applies here. You take direction from those ahead of you. Never from those behind you.

When it comes to feedback, you should listen *only* to people ahead of you. This means it's coming from someone ahead of you in terms of knowledge, success, or expertise. It's genuine insight that's coming from a place of true lived experience and applicable wisdom. These are the masters of your craft, the people you look up to, the teachers you respect, and the people who have accomplished what you want to do. If they are ahead of you *and* you respect them, then bingo. You're all ears.

When you have feedback that's coming from someone behind you, it's from folks who are not doing big, bold things with their lives. This includes internet trolls eating a bag of Doritos and typing with their cheesy fingers in the basement of their mother's house and annoying people who give unsolicited advice from no place of experience. Don't listen to anyone who isn't putting themselves out there to be judged.

If someone ahead of me who has a number one *New York Times* best-selling book, like Elizabeth Gilbert, gave me advice on a better way to write a chapter, I'd shut up immediately and haul out my notebook. She's currently sold twelve million copies of *Eat Pray Love* and, as of now, I'm still typing this damn thing. If my editor or agent suggested that I change the title, I'd listen. They've been in the business almost as long as I've been alive. They are ahead of me in terms of publishing experience and I trust 'em. If Jen freaking Sincero offered me an hour of her time to advise me, I'd fangirl and show up, like, an hour early.

But if some annoying chick sends me a long email with her opinions on how I should do my book (even though she has zero books of her own), then I don't listen. When in doubt (and when the feedback really stings), ask yourself: Is this person ahead of me or behind me?

There is one important caveat here: recurring input from your *paid* customers is always valuable feedback. (Notice I said "paid"? No skin in the game = no listening from you.) If many students tell me that module three of my online course isn't clear, I'll change it. They are showing up, investing in themselves, and doing the work. They've got skin in the game. But if some random looky-loo (who's never bought my course) wants to tell me that my modules are misordered, then I don't give a rat's ass.

Don't waste time listening to people who don't know what it's like to go for your dream.

Part 4

The New Playbook for Success

Because you're a genius now, you need some new rules to play by. Hustling 'til you get a stress ulcer doesn't cut it anymore in the new paradigm.

chapter 23

Your Best Success Will Come from What's Most Profoundly Simple

Last summer, my friend and I were sitting around the table, eating sushi and listening to some old '70s jams, including the Eagles' "Take It Easy." I was busy stuffing my face with avocado rolls when my friend said, "Gosh, that was such a simple song. I could have written that."

First, I hate when people say this sorta crap. Because ya didn't. And second . . .

Only a master can make it easy because it takes a genius to make something simple.

That song is a great example. It takes a lot of talent to strike that level of simplistic brilliance. And that kind of ability can only be accomplished by those who are really grounded in their gifts.

It's taken me years of mastery to take one huge concept—building a full-time business from finding your genius and monetizing it—and break it down into a simple step-by-step process. While it may look easy for me to teach a course or for Gwyneth Paltrow to crank out the next hit clean-eating cookbook or for Piet Mondrian to create abstract art with primary colors and black lines, it's years in the making.

So, while you think stuff looks "easy," you're really just watching a master at their craft. (Or, as I would say, a genius.)

What does this mean for you? Your best success will come from what's most profoundly simple. The kicker is that your highest expression of genius will be natural for you and you won't have to work hard at it. The key thing is not to screw that up when it happens.

Let me tell you the story of how I *did* screw this up.

When I was working on one of my tech start-ups in Silicon Valley, I was hustling night and day. The idea was to reclaim organic, soon-to-expire food that grocery stores usually dump too soon when, in fact, it could be consumed today. I was also offering the "ugly produce" that farmers compost because stores wanna sell only the pretty stuff. The goal was to build a subscription-model food delivery service aimed at scoring wholesale prices on wholesome organic grub. There were many red flags. One, I absolutely suck at logistics, and the idea of thinking that *okay, this food needs to get picked up from this store and needs to get delivered to this person . . . all while staying cold . . . and properly labeled . . . and fresh . . .* just makes my brain want to melt into mush. Two, this was not profoundly simple for me or aligned with my genius. I wasn't speaking, teaching, or connecting. I was creating, but it was the *wrong* dang creation. Three, I could not code an app or find someone to do it, which left me trying to learn C++ and other bizarre languages of the internet and giving up fast.

To conduct research, I did everything from dumpster diving to eating expired food. Because grocery store managers wouldn't tell me how much food waste was getting tossed, I snuck around at night and climbed into their disposal bins myself. And if you want to potentially sell food that's going to be tossed, ya might as well see how bad it really is, right?

I once got so accidentally sick from eating some seriously expired hummus that I took a last-minute flight out of SFO, paid the extra $200 surcharge, and got my ass back to Canada, where the health care is free, because I didn't know what weird worm (or bug or other dumpster-dwelling parasite) I'd picked up. Diarrhea + ungodly small plane bathrooms + turbulence + people knocking on the door to ask if I'm okay = worst two hours of my life.

Skip the tummy troubles and take it from me: your best success will come from what's most profoundly simple.

I'll contrast the embarrassment that ensued with how simple it is for me to make money from my current business. All I have to do is crack open my laptop, work with a client for an hour, and answer all their business questions. Easy as pie, fun, and a total no-brainer for me. Plus, clients pay me real-deal money for my time. When I was dumpster diving in the garbage bins of San Francisco and running to the toilet, I made zero. Everything about my start-up was just straight-up hard. I didn't have the skill set to make it work, I had no freaking clue what I was really doing, and it felt like I was meeting roadblock after roadblock.

When you're leveraging your greatest gifts, it isn't hard. Sure, parts of any endeavor are going to be challenging and you'll have problems that are a pain in the ass, but you'll feel internally compelled to pursue it. It feels like a "want to" versus a "have to."

Don't make the same mistake as me and aim to do the hardest, weirdest, stupidest stuff. Skip that and let your success be simple. Everyone benefits when it's easier for you to produce and you actually enjoy it. You'll be happier, your clients will be happier, your coworkers will be happier, and your therapist will be too.

Things to remember when you're tempted to eat the expired hummus for research purposes:

- When I hit a rough patch or I notice that I'm dragging ass, I ask myself: *Is this profoundly simple for me or am I rummaging around through the garbage bins at night?*
- Where are you metaphorically dumpster diving in your own life? What's something you dread? And how can you commit to finding success from something profoundly simple instead?
- Success doesn't need to be complicated. The best creations are all innately simple. Every time I wanna go make things harder than they need to be, I remember that some of the things I enjoy most are ridiculously simple. Like my iPhone's design, peanut butter and jelly, and the Eagles' "Take It Easy" (which is a very fitting name).
- You can judge a master's ability by how easily they can make something simple. Where are you able to make things simple in your life? How can you spend more time doing that?

chapter 24

Nobody Else Can Do It Like You (No Matter How Hard They Try)

Do you know someone who's just so dang awesome at what they do? They are, like, annoyingly good. You respect them, of course, but you're also like, *Damn, how do I get on that level?*

Back in the day, whenever I met a successful person, I was always trying to crack the code on what they were doing and how exactly they got that way. I could never really put my finger on it. Or get on their level. There was this guy named Lucas at university. He was gregarious and fun, could strike up a convo with any stranger, and always gave a five-star presentation in every goddamn class. *How is this even possible? I don't know.* To boot, he got a full scholarship to do his master's at Oxford and dressed impeccably well. Essentially, he was all the things. My most vivid memory of him was when he invited me to a TED-style talk and somehow the speakers invited him for drinks after it ended, even though we were sitting in the back row. And he was technically still underage at the time.

I was always like, *What the heck, man? How do I become like you?*

I saw Lucas as the pinnacle of success. Cool. Sophisticated. Had his shit together. So I tried to pull a page from his book and apply it to my own life. Yet, whenever I tried to be slick like him and invite speakers to get coffee with me, it came off as weird. They'd be like, "Uh, send me an email and my assistant will get in touch." Which is code for fuck off. By trying harder to be like Lucas, I had outcomes that were even worse. How ironic, because I thought mimicking him would make me more successful.

It took me a long time to figure it out. It was only once I gave up the well-intentioned copying and started doing things my way that it clicked.

You're either the genius or the copycat. You can't be both.

Since the dawn of time, the follow-the-leader approach has been the most commonly taught method for advancement. And, in my opinion, it's complete garbage. It's usually about trying to copy someone else's genius and pawn it off as your own. "Follow my ten steps!" "Do it like the textbook says!" "You can be just like me for only $9.99!"

I hate to admit it, but I did this for years. I did this with Lucas and with anybody I deemed accomplished. I taught stuff like my coaches did instead of leaning into my own style. I modeled other people's start-ups when structuring mine. At the heart of it, I was a huge copycat.

I was so afraid of getting it wrong that I played "monkey see, monkey do." I always thought that whatever other people were doing was better than whatever I had going on. Because I was desperately afraid of failing, I did a lot of duplicating.

Now, there is a time and a place to follow the road map. Like when you follow the instructions on how to assemble the IKEA bookshelf so you can (hopefully) avoid having a nervous breakdown. Or when you get coaching so you can learn from the folks who went before you. Yet there's an intuitive fine line between following the leader and copying them so much that your genius fades out because you're trying so hard to "get it right."

You can't follow your own genius when you're busy trying to be a copycat.

You gotta trust that the way you do things is right. Geniuses march to the beat of their own drum. They do things their own way and don't think twice about how the outside world perceives them. Like Lucas, when he started chatting up the circle of speakers standing outside the main doors of the theater. He didn't ask for permission or consult me about whether this was a good idea or not. He just waltzed over there and said howdy.

You're either doing your own thing and rocking your genius unapologetically . . . or you're Ctrl+C and Ctrl+V-ing your résumé from something stellar you saw online and tweaking a few words with a thesaurus. Trying to be like someone else is the surest way to always come in second place. Instead, your best outcome will occur when you lean into your authentic essence.

Now, are you ready for the twist?

The huge cosmic joke was that I used to be a copycat. Then, once I leaned into my genius, people started to copy me.

I lost a lotta sleep over the competitors who ripped off my ideas, or whose sales pages looked too much like mine, or who also suddenly called themselves experts in the "find your genius and monetize it" space. (Which is my methodology and phrasing. I guess I should buy some more trademarks.) It honestly drove me bonkers. *Would they poach my clients? Would my students jump ship and move their community? Or, dare I say, what if these copycats suddenly got super successful and eclipsed me? What if they'd take my ideas and I'd be stuck in the dust?*

Here's what you need to know: nobody else can do it like you, no matter how hard they try. You have something special that everyone else covets and wants to imitate. Believe me, it's there. And when you do that thing, nobody can hold a candle to you.

I couldn't be like Lucas, no matter how many speakers I tried to schmooze. And my copycats couldn't coach exactly like me no matter how much their websites looked like mine.

Your genius can't be duplicated or manufactured. A robot can't replace your gifts and there is no algorithm that can match your je ne sais quoi. People may try to mirror and clone it, but they can't.

Your genius is a unique expression of your own soul, and the way you express it is unique to you. Nobody can replace you, mimic it, or rip you off. They simply can't do it like you, no matter how hard they try.

The copycats will fizzle out because copying someone else's genius and claiming it as your own isn't exactly a winning formula for innovation. It can only take you so far because when it comes time to create something new or change strategy, only the OG—and not the original gangster, the original genius—can do that successfully. So, as you go about your soul's calling, you don't need to worry about competitors stealing business away or Suzie from work ripping off your idea. Even if she does, it won't be as good as yours because it's not coming from the core essence of her being. I mean, look: We all know that the black-market Louis Vuitton isn't the same as the real one. And that the Elvis impersonator, no matter how good the wig, isn't Elvis.

Lastly, a genius knows that nobody can knock off their "it factor," because it's not just a final result or a product—it's the articulation of their own soul. The way you do things also stems from your red thread, trials, and tribulations. This goes back to what I said before: you are the competitive advantage. All you need is yourself. And you've had it all along.

Lean into the genius that only you embody.

Genius	Copycat
• Trusts their gifts, quirks, and genius.	• Doesn't trust their gifts and apologizes for their quirks.
• Paves their own way and takes creative risks.	• Follows in others' footsteps and plays by the book.
• Says, "Screw it! I'm doing it like this!"	• Buys into the myth that you have to follow a certain way of doing things.
• Is willing to think for themselves.	• Has an "I'll have what she's having" mentality.
• Follows intuitive impulses and experiments.	• Is scared of failing, so they steal other people's ideas.
• Has high self-worth.	• Has low self-worth.
• Is willing to take risks if there is a chance of success.	• Is preoccupied with fear of failure.
• Trusts that the way they do things is right.	• Thinks other people are doing it "better."
• Doesn't care if you like them. Knows their products or services are for a specific group of people.	• Wants to be everything to everybody.
• Asks: "How should I do this? What feels right for me?" Turns inward for answers.	• Asks: "How are other people approaching this?" Looks outward for answers, especially at what's been done before.
• Doesn't give a shit what others are doing.	• Constantly compares themselves with other people and wonders how they stack up.
• Can innovate and bring something new to the world.	• Has nothing unique to say. Offers a hodgepodge of what's been done before.
• Does it in their own style for the goal of creative expression and self-actualization.	• Mimics others' style or craft for the sake of "getting it right."

chapter 25

Quitting Is Underrated

The most defining moments in my life occurred when I intentionally quit something that was expensive, prestigious, difficult to attain, or societally perceived as "awesome" in order to follow the light of my own North Star.

I've quit many things.

On my very first day of employment at the local pet shop, when I was sixteen, I was shadowing the boss on the cash register and shelf-stocking duties. It was my friend's birthday party the next day and I didn't want to miss it, so I just quit. (I guess I've always had an issue with authority.)

I've quit internships only one week into starting them, I've walked away from fancy programs, and I've left high-level coaching mastermind groups that cost $40,000. I've fired new hires within the first week, I've walked away from three businesses, and I quit my full-time job after college four months before it even started.

I quit early and I quit often.

I've ended first dates saying, "God, you are so hot with those puppy-dog brown eyes and you look just like John Mayer, but I don't think this is going to go anywhere." And I'm the kind of person who will straight-out leave the spin class five minutes in if I don't like the music or instructor, regardless of if I've paid twenty-five bucks for the class.

Average joes and other rule followers are always like, "What? You're leaving?"

Quitting is underrated.

What is the point of slogging it out in something you hate? I don't think there is anything cool or impressive about grinding away at something you absolutely loathe. Instead, I celebrate quitting. It's a lesson in liberation. Quitting lets you free up your time so that you can do what you're really meant to do. When you say no to something that's not in alignment with who you really are, then you make space for what's meant for you.

Yet quitting is one of the most unpopular and polarizing options. Very similar to pineapple on pizza. A lot of people freak out when I suggest it. Quitting, that is.

Here's a frequent example: Clients will call me in a panic and rattle on about how they hate their job and their boss and their commute and their coworkers and how freaking Sarah from sales leaves her dishes in the goddamn communal kitchen sink all the time.

I'll say, "Okay, then quit."

They reply, "But I need to stay here a full year to make my résumé cohesive!"

Or, "But if I stay six more years, I get a pension!"

Or, "But I love the extended health care package! I mean, I don't need eye care, but I might later."

I give a lot of people the advice to straight-up quit, and based on their reactions, I don't think they like it. Quitting usually comes off as cringeworthy because you're going up against everything society taught you. (Put in the time! Earn your stripes! Climb the ladder!) Conventional wisdom suggests that quitting too soon is a sign of weakness. It's like you gave up, or you didn't give enough of a concerted effort or didn't try hard enough. (Give it more time, you'll come around to it. You've been at that job for only a month. It's too soon to tell.)

Sometimes you know on day one. So, why stay until day 365?

Perhaps leaving your job makes you feel like you're admitting defeat, waving your white flag. Or maybe it makes you feel like a quitter, even though you're usually able to stick with things long term. Or maybe you worry about how you'll explain the yearlong gap in your résumé to your next interviewer. At the end of the day, geniuses don't make decisions based on other people's reactions because they honor their own intuition instead. **Sure, you might let people down if you leave early, but you'll let yourself down if you leave too late.**

Quitting is one of the most courageous things you can do with your life. To acknowledge when something isn't working and pull the plug is the epitome of personal power. It's about knowing what you stand for, what you will tolerate, and what you will accept. It's about respecting your own time and energy. You don't have to keep staying in something that's not serving you. (This goes for other non-career-related things, too, like relationships or sitting in the sauna for too long when your face already looks like a tomato.)

When you know it's time to quit, it becomes a feeling that's hard to ignore. But if you wait around hemming and hawing . . . and spend more hours flossing your teeth while debating the situation . . . then your inner critic will get in there and screw the whole thing up. It will dissuade you from leaping off the proverbial diving board and get you to climb back down the stairs. When, in fact, it would have been easier if you'd just jumped.

Taking swift, decisive action disrupts this pattern. This ensures that you quit the stuff that isn't working for you *and* that you're not backing out of your genius ideas simply because they feel scary or unfamiliar.

Waiting, stalling, and buying time are not hallmarks of high self-worth. So the best way to honor your genius and dump the crap that's misaligned is to craft a "no-do" list. This is where you outline all the shit you hate, all the stuff that isn't a full-body "hell yes," and all the "shoulds" you feel expected to do in order to please others. Don't hold back. Write down tasks you despise, errands that drain you, clients that sound like Scrooge—or whatever it is for you. Then give yourself a short time frame (from twenty-four hours to one month) to say no to everything. (Yes, everything.)

For big things, you are picking a date and holding yourself accountable. For example, if you need to quit a job, give yourself a deadline, like resigning in six months. The key is to choose a date *now*. So haul out your calendar and decide when your last day will be. Once the deadline is in place, you have a runway and can begin mapping out a strategy. That includes getting your savings to float you for several months, building up your business now, and planning for how you'll make money in your newly found free time.

For pesky tasks, ask yourself: How can I automate this, delegate this, or eliminate it entirely? If it's not in your genius, you have to pick one of the three.

For small things, fire them off ASAP. If you need to have a hard conversation, do it now. If you need to notify Scrooge that you won't renew his contract, email him by the end of the day. Whenever you attempt something tenacious, your inner critic is going to deceive you into thinking this is a bad idea (even though you got confirmation from your heart that it's the right choice), so you need to act fast.

The major key to the "no-do" list is speed.

Less time = less shit you have to deal with from your inner critic.

Longer deadlines = higher probability that you won't complete your goal.

And look, quitting ain't that bad. When you are walking your true journey in life and you have the courage to leave something big behind, unexpected opportunities show up. These may come in the form of a mentor who appears when the student is ready or a job with your name on it at just the right time. Every time I left something big behind, I got rewarded on the other side: my mastermind group for this book, my full-time job for my wild ride in Silicon Valley, my unsavory summer internship for an opportunity at Tesla, my first job for my friend's sweet sixteen birthday-party sleepover. (Okay, fine. Not the last one, but you see what I'm saying.)

You just gotta trust that you will be rewarded on the other side. Will it all show up on day one? No. But if you keep walking, one day it will.

Things to remember when you're reciting the "to quit or not to quit" soliloquy in your head:

- Down the road, when you are all successful 'n' stuff, people will glorify you for going for it. They will call you a maverick and an icon. But at the start, they might question the shit out of you and think you're absolutely dumber than a bag of nails. For example, the same person who told me I was brilliant for doing this book also gave me one of those sit-down are-you-sure-you-know-what-you're-doing kinda talks when I said I wanted to try a fourth business. Which ultimately led me to the book.

- If it ain't working, stop. You have the permission to quit.

- People spend years planning how they'll quit or start something, when in fact it's disadvantageous to delay. If you take a month to debate whether your website branding should be blue or brown, your inner critic is going to think, *Gosh, this is all stupid. You can't do this.* And then you'll never have a business and the moment will never arise for you to actually choose your colors. Planning can be a clever stall tactic and discreetly devised deception that prevents you from pursuing your genius.

- One final note: when you are in your genius, you will *not* want to quit. In fact, the universe might hurl everything at you and you will still keep going, like Tom Hanks on his raft in *Cast Away*. Your genius will require undying devotion. The kind of devotion that comes with the stings and the sorrows from the relentless commitment to the pursuit of your own heart. Your genius might take you to the depths of your being and challenge you consistently, but you just won't quit. You won't want to. You'll love it so much that you won't be willing to wave your white flag. And that's how you'll know you've hit it.

chapter 26

Your Genius Makes You One of a Kind

Your genius makes you one of a kind because nobody else can do certain things like you can. At work, this is how you become the first pick for the team and the last one they'll ever fire. In your business, this is how you get loyal customers and oodles of referrals. In life, this is how you become magnetic, irreplaceable, and the only option in people's eyes.

When you do *your* thing in *your* way, it produces that "it factor" that people talk about. And you suddenly become head and shoulders above everybody else.

Let me share three real-world examples of one-of-a-kind geniuses I've stumbled upon.

I used to work with Kathy at the pool. She taught all the advanced lifeguarding classes and was a lifeguard for more than twenty years. If there was a drowning swimmer, she was first in the water. If some toddler pooped in the pool, she was immediately on the scene to take care of it. No fuss. No commotion. Just calm, cool, and collected. One day, she told us a horrifying story about how she was giving this guy mouth-to-mouth and he puked in her mouth . . . and she still kept going and saved him. I mean, lifeguard of the year award or what? How could you ever fire a person like that? Never.

I went to school with a guy named Naheel. He had the most creative ideas. I swear to god that brilliance would pour out of his mouth. I'd be trying to think of a marketing strategy, and he'd just wow everyone with a whole new idea. He was also cool. Danced hip-hop, made a Drake coloring book, and also got scooped up by Google after college. Naheel was the kind of person you aspired to be like and the one you'd make eye contact with when the professor said, "Now, you'll have to find yourself a team for this project . . ."

I stayed at this Airbnb on the Amalfi Coast and the owner, Alessi, was your dream host. She was a fashion designer, the property had been in her family for years, and she made the whole ocean-facing villa just impeccable. It looked like it was from the pages of *Vogue Italia*. She thought of everything. From the hand-painted ceramic logo on the front door to the housekeeper who came once a day to make our beds to the shampoo that smelled like the lemons of Italy. You could tell that taking care of her guests was what she was born to do. This was the kind of experience that you wanted to keep coming back to every year. And the one to recommend to all your friends.

When you do your genius, you become first-class at your own craft. Whatever your talent is, there's a dent in the universe with your name on it. Whether you're a mathematician or a whiz at making vegetables taste good, your gifts matter. There's space for you. Even if you find yourself wondering, *Who the heck cares about the way I fold socks and tidy drawers?* Actually, many will. And usually more than you even realize. I mean, look how we desperately needed the life-changing magic of Marie Kondo's genius. But you only find out if you take the leap. Your genius is needed. In whatever way you express it. And the more niche/weird/specialized, the better. Because it makes you one of a kind.

chapter 27

Trying Harder Doesn't Always Work

Have you ever stuck your finger in a finger trap? It was one of those bad birthday-party loot bag gifts you'd receive as a kid when you really just wanted a strawberry ring pop and a dollar-store candy necklace. The irony is that the harder you tug to pull your fingers out of the trap, the tighter it becomes. Despite being a highly alarming toy for a small child and a tearjerker at the end of a fun birthday party, the point is that you've gotta let go and relax to become free. The same thing goes for success; it's not about the frantic push to the finish line, but rather about flow, ease, and alignment.

Counterintuitive? Yes.

Wrong? No.

The truth about life is that trying harder doesn't always work. Look, the pathway to your dreams is not all unicorns 'n' rainbows and all the marshmallows from the box of Lucky Charms with none of the cereal. It's anything but. Yet you'll always be rewarded at some point along the journey.

For many years of my life, I never saw the fruits of my labor. It was like all cereal and no freaking charms. I desperately wanted my three former start-ups to work out. But I made zero dollars. I wanted cool companies to hire me. But none seemed to want me.

And there was one company I had my eye on for years that I could not get a job at. It's a little Vancouver-based company. Maybe you know it? Lululemon Athletica? (I'm joking. Of course, you know it.) Well, I wanted a job there. *Badly.* Every summer, I applied for their internships. Nada. During the school year, I applied to work retail. It was always a no. Even in their stores, I got rejected four times to fold pants. And one year while I was living in Paris I decided to do something different. Instead of sending a PDF with my résumé and cover letter for a coveted internship at the head office, I built a whole website called yolululemon.com that included a list of my ten-year goals and a page dedicated to how I'd elevate the company as an intern with new, cool ideas for the brand. I even filmed a fun, spunky video that featured me running around the streets of Paris in a neon-pink Lululemon jacket, talking about why I'd be a good pick for the position. I didn't even get a callback for an interview.

It was almost preposterous. I had straight As, all the extracurriculars, connections at the company, a good personality, sweet references from my professors, and still, I couldn't get hired at their head office.

Sometimes not getting what you want can be the best thing that ever happened to you. And everything that you do contributes to your final destination even if you're failing 'n' fucking it up right now. But I was a nimnod and didn't know that. One of my mentors just told me to "trust the process." At that point in my life, I would rather have learned how to swallow swords than learn how to do that.

I wasn't going to trust the process. So I tried to control it.

I tried harder to get hired by the purveyor of black stretchy pants. I sent out more résumés. I networked more. Took more people for coffee, or lunch, or a drink if that's what they wanted. I tried asking Lululemon employees at the head office if I could take them for yoga and green juice. I tried ramping up my efforts and doubling down. I tried pouring in more hours. Practicing different interview questions. Sending crazier résumés to get noticed. Along with creating that website from Paris, I had a French baguette and raspberry jam delivered to the recruiter's office with a note that said, "Bonjour! I'm Kelly! I want to be your next intern."

I did anything I could think of to get what I wanted. And, truth be told, this was how the rest of my life looked too.

Control was my default coping mechanism. I had my life planned out to a tee. I wanted to be on the 8 a.m. bus, sit in my favorite spot on the left-hand side by the window, and arrive to class five minutes early. I wanted to be in a high-paying job by twenty-five, have a sleek blonde ponytail with no flyaways at all times, and own a ritzy downtown condo by thirty. (But don't sit on my white leather couch with your blue jeans on. It will stain.) I wanted the upper hand on which flight my boyfriend and I were booking and what type of hand soap we were buying. If I felt a breakup coming, I'd break up first. If the weather forecast said that there was a 30 percent chance of precipitation, I'd have an umbrella on me. (Because god forbid my hair got wet.) And don't you dare try to throw me a surprise birthday party. (Control freaks *hate* surprise parties.)

To be in your genius and really rock it, you need to let go, trust, and surrender. These were my three least favorite things a few years ago. Your genius has an intuitive nature to it, which means you're in the zone, you're following the flow, you're not really thinking, you're just doing. It's very hard to be present in the moment if you're always trying to control it.

Control is being in your head. Surrender is being in your body.

Control is forcing. Surrender is allowing.

Control is thinking you know best. Surrender is knowing you don't.

At the end of the day, here's how I define surrender: relaxing into the outcome, loosening the grip, not worrying too much about the final result, not fretting over the "how" and the "when" 24/7. Surrendering means letting go of the previewed path and living life with an open palm. No wonder it's so foreign to follow your genius when we're accustomed to controlling our lives by climbing the ladder, paying attention to the rules, and trying not to trip up by accidentally making something new.

After four years of trying to get a job at Lululemon, I walked away with nothing. When I finally let go, gave up, and accepted another internship, I got a text from an old coworker from my magazine intern days. "Looking for summer work? I have a part-time internship for you on my team! I just switched jobs and I'm now at Lululemon." (FYI, I never ended up working at the head office. I was already halfway through an internship somewhere else.) My point is that the second you give up, the universe surprises you. The same thing goes for the finger trap. You gotta let go to be free. So tell your inner critic to shut up and try surrendering sometimes. It really works.

Things to remember when you're resending your résumé for the five hundredth time to Lululemon (or whatever your version of the story is):

- Perhaps this is the time to answer the harder question: Why are you trying so hard to control this outcome? Are you afraid of uncertainty, failure, or looking bad? Are you scared of letting go because you only know what it's like to hold on?
- If you find yourself struggling to score some serious momentum for a prolonged period of time, then it might be a sign that you're totally off your genius. The pursuit of your genius should

have a dimension of flow to it. As in, something's gotta give. If it's one big grind and all uphill, then you're missing the mark.

- Nikola Tesla said the secrets of the universe are in frequency, energy, and vibration. And when you are banging your head against the wall at the eleventh hour, that ain't exactly the same as being in that high-vibe flow. You have no cool frequency when you're flogging yourself with work at 2 a.m. When you're stuck, ask yourself: What's flowing to me in the present moment? What would be the most fun thing to do right now? Listen to what the muse is telling you.

- Sometimes the opposite is the answer. When you've been staring at the blank Google doc for the last hour and you still have writer's block, don't keep sitting there. If you can't effing get a job at Lululemon despite your absurd number of attempts, maybe take it as a sign to stop. Trying harder isn't always the solution. Yet surrender usually is. Always look in the opposite direction if you're not getting the results you want.

chapter 28

Choose Exponential Results over Incremental Gains

Many old-timey business books give the advice that you gotta "build the wall brick by brick." When I read these, I think, *Oh c'mon. Where's the fun in that? Where's the fast-forward button so I can get to the good stuff?*

You see, I love speed. I listen to all podcasts at double speed and I climb all stairs two at a time. I walk fast, I eat fast, I type fast, I work fast, and I want everything to happen fast. "Slow 'n' steady" sounds like a great late-night playlist for some sexy time, but a lousy way to make a living in my opinion.

One day, I came across the concept of making a quantum leap. Scientifically speaking, a quantum leap is when an atom abruptly changes its state and "jumps" from one level to another, kinda out of nowhere. It happens instantly and somehow uses no effort. It's some weird, freaky science shit. According to some old books from the '80s, I could apparently do this with my life too. The process involved part action (I was already great at taking action) and part magic (heck yeah, I wanted some magic).

You see, I'm a crystal-hoarding, metaphysical-book-loving kinda gal. So this idea of making things serendipitously appear in your life magically versus manually sounded perfect. (For real, though, mantras and visualizations would be a piece of cake compared to actually doing the work and sucking up to important people in itchy wool suits.) Needless to say, I bought the books, documented the recommended actions, and diligently did them for thirty days.

Here's how it went. After breakfast, lunch, and dinner, I had to excuse myself and perform my strange list of tasks. To start, I had to write down everything I was grateful for while listening to fist-pumping music for twenty minutes. The instructions were to choose precisely twenty gratitudes. No more, no less. Next, I needed to visualize my biggest goal and get so emotional and worked up about it that I could cry tears of joy (which was encouraged). Then, I had to read a list of cheesy-ass affirmations like "I love money and money loves me" while making eye contact with myself in the mirror. Lastly, I was to conclude by declaring the mantra "My quantum leap is coming" to seal the deal. I was instructed to erase all disbelief and expect that somehow, someway, a radical shift would occur. The weirdos who wrote these kinds of books also said this was a strict process and if you screwed up, then you'd have to start all over again to reach thirty days. (Which I hate because you know on day eighteen you're going to forget.)

What's my point? You can get a quantum leap by forgoing the mantras. Harnessing your genius is just as effective. Instead of wasting your time crying tears of joy (three times a day, I might add), simply commit to doing more stuff that's centered on your greatest gifts. Anyone can instantaneously "jump" from one level to another when they are doing the work they were born to do.

Applying your genius is a lot like math. What's more effective—using addition or exponents? If two people are given the same input of 10, but use a different method of math, they can get a vastly different result.

Here's the breakdown:

$10 + 10 = 20$
$10^2 = 100$

Most people only know how to make marginal gains in their lives. They are stuck doing 10 + 10. (Improve your weaknesses by taking a course. Ask for a 2 percent annual raise. Learn the Excel keyboard short-cuts to save five minutes of formatting.) Only geniuses know how to take the same input of 10 and square it to make 100.

Now, before we talk about going fast, let's talk about what it's like to go slow. This is also known as improving your weaknesses, like your college counselor advised you to do. When you go slow, it's like add-ing 10 + 10—like me in a GPA-eating class called Quantitative Decision Making. Essentially, you had to learn how to color-code a spreadsheet in primary colors, crunch numbers, and figure out the optimal output a factory should produce based on some formula I forgot the second the semester ended.

I *sucked* at this class.

Although I worked on the homework with my three roommates (so that I could bum answers off them), I had to practice on my own to pass the test. It was strenuous and gagworthy. When I got bored studying in the library, I closed the textbook and yanked out my phone to go on Tinder, swipe around, and message the hotties. (Real story of how I met my college boyfriend.)

Doing crap that wasn't in alignment with my genius felt like doing mathematical addition. I could only get marginally better. Instead of having trouble doing six out of ten of the homework questions, I had issues with only five. My test scores moved from 61 percent to 63 percent. Everything was an incremental gain. It was like pulling teeth because no matter how hard I tried, I still sucked.

Now, let's look at the opposite. When you leverage your genius, your results increase exponentially. The more you lean into your edges, the bigger the payoff. And the more devotion you pour in, the higher the exponential return. You'll go from being amazing to fuckin' fantastic. When you're tapped into your genius, you can simply do more, create more, and produce way better stuff. This is how you take that same input of 10 and turn it into 100.

I noticed this pattern occurring in my life. As I spent more time speaking, teaching, creating, and connecting, I became exponentially better at each of those things. For example, I went from stumbling and scripting every sentence of my podcast to free-flowing an hour's worth of content off the top of my head and talking into a microphone to thousands of people like it was no big deal.

And then, one day, it happened: I made my first financial quantum leap and earned $25,000 in eleven days. For a girl who originally started a blog and sold a $19 e-book with two swear words in the title, this was a lot of money. It was the first time I realized I was onto something big.

To generate exponential results, you need to make a major modification in the way you operate. This means forgoing a yawn-inducing linear path to growth. Instead, it's about thinking differently and challenging your perceptions. If you wanna go where you've never been before, then you've gotta do something you've never done before. You can't keep doing the same shit day in and day out and expect your life to be wildly different. Instead, you have to be willing to pursue your goals in a radically different way rather than sticking to the same method you've been using.

When I made that $25,000 in eleven days, I was doing all sorts of stuff I had never done before. For starters, I shelled out some serious moolah for coaching and I did whatever the hell the coach said because I had just forked over a huge wad of cash. I pivoted my offerings, changed prices, rewrote pages, created new marketing plans, tried different sales strategies, and did almost everything differently. I narrowed my niche and solemnly swore to do only a specific type of business coaching so that I could be ridiculously dialed into my genius. Lastly, I was speaking, teaching, creating, and connecting more than I ever had in my whole life. I was doing my genius (and selling it) like it was goin' outta style.

As humans, we usually stay within the bounds of what we already know how to do, refuse to change, and then get frustrated when we feel like our usual song and dance isn't working.

Changing your strategy might feel riskier than doing what you've always done. But "different" doesn't always mean "risky." And "unfamiliar" shouldn't always be swapped for "scarier." Nothing I did was that ludicrous. Rewriting your sales pages isn't exactly like getting your tongue pierced and dropping everything to tour with your rock 'n' roll band.

Here's the perspective flip I want you to have:

Old narrative: risky + scary
Example: skydiving without a parachute
Thought: *holy mutherfucking crap*
Result: you'll never wanna do it

New narrative: different + unfamiliar
Example: going to Spain for the first time
Thought: *I could manage that*
Result: something you can totally warm up to

An easy way to swap incremental gains for exponential results is to relinquish your regular confines of thinking and try something new. Seek solutions that will propel you forward in a major way, but are not so preposterous that you wanna spit out your water when you hear them. It doesn't need to be this wild, crazy, blow-all-your-money gambling spree in Vegas. What you do just needs to be different from what you've always done.

Here are some different (but not risky) examples:

- Finding an investor versus funding it yourself
- Getting a mentor versus Googling forever
- Dropping off your résumé in person with a handwritten note attached versus emailing it like everyone else
- Selling your hand-knit hats online versus only at the local farmers market
- Making an online dating profile to expand the number of people you reach versus solely attending Singles Night at the local library hoping you'll find your soul mate
- Asking all your customers "Do you want fries with that?" as a way to make more income versus hoping they'll order 'em on their own
- Chatting up every one of your Uber passengers to make new connections and tell 'em your dream of becoming a sitcom actor versus saying nothing the whole time

Lastly, be on the lookout for anything serendipitous that will advance you forward. When you're focused on the end goal of living your genius, you'll bump into random "hows" that present themselves and look like a pathway to your final destination. I call this a "quantum how" because it answers the "how" part of your goal when you had no freaking clue how you'd get there. If it flows to you in an unexpected way through an unexpected source, and if it feels like a mini-miracle, then take it. This is your ticket to an exponential result.

Be willing to leap when the opportunity appears. This means if your Uber passenger says they are a famous director and they ask for your business card . . . *give them your card*!

I'm no scientist, but this could be the leap you've been looking for.

chapter 29

Throw Out Everything You Know and Go with How It Feels

"Welcome to the Universe! How may I take your order?"

Did you know you have a totally free 24/7 hotline where you can get answers to all your burning questions without ever having to put a coin in a pay phone? You can place an order anytime and no request is too small. You can even keep calling back a million times and the voice on the other side will gladly help you out, rather than pretending that the manager isn't in the building.

This is called tapping into your intuition.

Your intuition is a deep well of wisdom inside you. It's the thing that knows if something is good or bad. It's your insight, gut reaction, or foresight. It's also known as your wise inner voice and some people call it the sound of whatever deity they choose. This connection is open any time—including holidays!—and you can get guidance whenever you'd like.

Now, much as we tend not to trust our genius, we *really* don't trust our intuition.

When I first heard this concept of connecting to your intuition, I was freaked out. Growing up, I heard a spooky story that if you leave a pad of paper out overnight and ask the ghost who lives in your house to write on it, they will leave their name. I was terrified of this. Yet very curious. So I left a pad of paper on the desk in my bedroom one night and told the ghost to do their thing. I thought that connecting to my intuition would be just like this. Would I hear eerie voices? Would I be connecting to my dead aunt through a Ouija board at midnight over the glow of a dim candle to get these answers? And thanks to my Catholic upbringing, I wondered if I'd be channeling the devil himself. Long story short, the paper was blank in the morning. All that panicking for nothing.

Turns out, listening to your intuition is a simple way to get practical advice. You've probably been doing it for years, so it's nothing to be nervous about. Your intuition is gentle and mellow. *You are the one who's been stressed.*

If you want to be a genius, you need to know how to tap into the innate wisdom inside you. You must develop the skill of looking inward for answers, following your own hunches, and doing what feels right for *you*, not what the salesperson wants (or what your mother wants, for that matter). You'll require the talent of trusting yourself, making decisions on your own, and being willing to listen to the voice inside when you wanna go left and everyone else is telling you to go right.

This is one of the biggest lessons I can teach you: sometimes, you have to throw out everything you know and go with how it feels. Regardless of what makes sense financially on the balance sheet, some matters of the heart can be solved only by looking inward. You can't always get the solution from a bar graph or a call to your mentor at 2 a.m. when you're tossing and turning at night over a big decision. But by dialing into your intuition? Absolutely.

The more you follow your genius and your intuition, the better things work out. So I'm going to teach you how to listen to it because it's reliable, instant, and, best of all, free.

Here's how to do it.

STEP 1: Know you have it.

You already have an intuition. Do you know that sensation of being in a creepy alley and getting that "Uhhhh, I gotta get outta here" feeling? You've felt it too? Okay, great, proceed to step two.

STEP 2: Figure out how you receive intuitive insight.

Everyone receives guidance in different ways. It depends on your spidey senses. I know this might sound like something for a psychic medium, but it's available to you too. So here are the five ways that you might be unknowingly connecting with your intuition on a daily basis.

1. **Seeing things.** (And no, this is not "I see dead people.") Your intuition comes to you in pictures. In your creative process, you might get visuals in your head for how you could film a video or design a room. These come as visions that flash across your mind. For me, I get images of how a client's business could look once we're done building it. I can just see it in my mind's eye. If you are a visual learner or you're good at visualizing the solution to a problem, those are also indicators that you could connect to your intuition this way. For example, an architect can just "see" how a home could be laid out in their mind as they're sketching it on paper.

2. **Hearing things.** This is when your intuition sounds like your own voice in your head, but more grounded, calm, and wise.

Your "inner voice" actually comes to you as a voice. Sometimes, you're like, *Who the hell said that? That's some real good shit right there. Let me get a pencil and jot this down* . . . This occurred when I heard the phrase "What if you just did what you were good at?" If this is how you connect with your intuition, then you'll hear bite-sized phrases that are straight to the point. If you're wrestling with a decision, try asking yourself a question, getting silent, and waiting to hear the answer. If you ask yourself, *Should I work with this client?* you will hear the word *yes* or *no* in your head. It's your own voice. Yet it's directed, pointed, and steady. If you are an auditory learner, listen up. You might have this connection in spades because you're already inclined to learn through sound. You likely are good at picking up information over the phone or love learning through podcasts. Personally, I learn best through audio. I coach my clients on the phone only (with no video) because I can understand them better and pick up on subtle cues from their voices alone. If you have a sharp connection to the sound of things, this might be an easy way to "hear" your intuition.

3. **Feeling things.** This is when you get a feeling in your body about something. Maybe you have a strong visceral reaction, get the chills, or have a gut feeling in your stomach. The body has infinite intelligence and it knows the truth of the matter before your head does. If you pay close attention, your body will give you a knee-jerk intuitive reaction to something. In your creative process, this surfaces as an overwhelming feeling from your gut that's like "OMG, yes!" when an idea is presented to you. Your heart races with excitement, electricity pumps through your veins, and you feel that buzz. Some describe it as "your heart leaping out of your chest." It's like your body is giving you the

green light. On the flip side, if you're getting the red light, you might feel physically sick or uncomfortable when presented with an option. Perhaps you might cry, clench your jaw, scratch nervously, or breathe shallowly. Your body language might start to close and you might unconsciously cross your arms or legs. When it comes to how our body reacts to a decision, here's a great example to think about: marriage proposals. When one person gets down on one knee, the other is either jumping for joy and squealing "YES!" or they're clamming up awkwardly and eyeing the easiest exit. Your body doesn't lie and that's why it can provide great insight into your true, deeper, intuitive feeling about the situation. Here's a personal example: I had this contract I was supposed to sign. Everything was fine and dandy. I nonchalantly talked to my lawyer about it many times, and when it was done, I was given a paper copy to sign. As I started reading it, I burst into uncontrollable tears. (Highly uncharacteristic of me even though I'm a sap for mushy movies.) This was a clear, visceral no. The more time you spend understanding how your body reacts to things, the more you'll witness subtle nuances. Knowing what a "yes" and a "no" feel like in your body will be particular to you. Understanding this enables you to make faster and better choices. If you are very connected to your body—maybe you do a lot of meditation or yoga—this might be an easy entry point to your intuition.

4. **Knowing things.** This is when we just "know" something, but can't really put words to why. Perhaps you have a premonition about something or you just "know" that investing all your money into your friend's new marijuana business will end poorly. Be careful here: if you have this gift, it's one of the easiest to ignore because you don't really have much to go by other than a strange

knowing. Your information can also come as a clear download or a relentless, nagging thought. Recently, I had a client who wanted to work with me. She was keen on making the investment, requested my most expensive package, and came as a referral from one of my favorite clients. She looked solid on paper, but I had a weird feeling about her. I couldn't exactly pinpoint what it was, but I had a feeling that if we worked together, it would end badly. Obviously, I had no evidence to prove this whatsoever. This is when you really need to throw out everything and go with how it feels. If you are good at knowing things without rhyme or reason, it just might be your intuition trying to connect with you.

5. **Smelling and tasting things.** Maybe you walk into a room and go, "Whoa, something smells off here." Or perhaps say something like, "This leaves me with a bad taste in my mouth." This means you have the ability to smell or taste things that give you insight into a situation even though they aren't physically in front of you.

Based on these descriptions, which ways of connecting with your intuition resonate most with you? You might have a few, so the more the merrier.

STEP 3: Practice with the small stuff.

Once you know how your intuition communicates with you, it's important to start practicing that connection. Before you ask serious life questions like "Should I pack all my belongings and become a nomad living out of an old orange Volkswagen bus?" start with the smaller stuff.

When it comes to teaching intuition, I always recommend clients start with the easy entry points: tomato sauce and your coffee order. Basically, things that are small choices under five bucks that have no huge implications or consequences.

For example, try standing in the grocery store in the tomato sauce section and let your intuition guide you to the right jar. If you're holding two different brands in each hand, go with your gut reaction. Don't hem and haw, either. Give yourself twenty seconds to choose because this will sharpen your intuitive connection.

If tomato sauce isn't your thing, no worries. Try your next coffee order. See what jumps out at you on the menu and lean into what you feel intuitively called toward. The key here is to *not* resist your impulses and instead let your mind take over. If you always order a large Americano, but today you're feelin' the London Fog, go for it. Honoring your intuition (and seeing a positive, delicious benefit) enables you to start trusting it. Because when you're happily sipping on that sweet London Fog in the bitter winter of New York, that sends a positive message to your brain: *trusting intuition = good*. Your brain works in simple language like that. Just like "Me Tarzan. You Jane." The goal is to prove to yourself that your intuition can guide you to the right answer. This forms a positive feedback loop in the brain.

Once you've mastered the basic level of tomato sauce and coffee, start asking questions about other everyday choices. Use "either/or" and "yes/no" questions. *Should I take the highway or the scenic route? Would this taste better if I added lemon or lime? Should I really be texting my ex again?* Once you ask, receive the answer in the way you connect with your sharpest senses. Maybe you'll see a visual of a lemon, hear the word *lemon* in your head, physically feel pulled toward the lemon, smell the scent, or taste it, or simply know that lemon is *obviously* the right choice for your meringue pie.

Look, I know this sounds like the weirdest thing ever and ten years ago I would have thought this stuff was totally quacky and equally as absurd as hauling out the Ouija board for answers.

Believe me, when you start living your authentic life and doing your genius, the questions are going to get harder. *Do I stay in my job or quit?*

Do I dump all my savings into this Malibu farmhouse and turn it into a retreat center? Do I take a risk and apply for that job in Madrid . . . or wonder what my life would be like if I never went for it? This is when you really need that input. Hard choices can't be solved through making a pros and cons list or a spreadsheet. And what happens if you ask all your trusted pals and they give you varied responses? It's annoying as heck. The easiest way to make hard choices is with your intuition. So build the muscle now.

STEP 4: Listen to your downloads.

So far, we've talked about listening to your intuition and tapping in when *you* wanna call the hotline. But how about when it's trying to get hold of you? Instead of sending a note attached to a pigeon's foot, the hotline reaches you by sending a "download" of information (aka an intuitive hit or suggestion). These come in the form of random thoughts, impulses, and action steps that feel as though they came outta the clear blue sky.

They can be as simple as the idea to drop by the bookstore to see if that book you want is back in stock yet. They can even be a handy tip for everyday life. Like the one I got last fall. One day, I had a random download to bring in my outdoor couch cushions. I dunno why. I made the mistake of brushing it off. In the middle of the night, the motion detector light went off and I scurried to the window. I was alarmed to see that the friendly neighborhood raccoon had decided that my couch was a good place to take a dump. Cut to me the next morning, decked out in yellow rubber gloves, angrily washing said cushions.

When it comes to these downloads, here are a few things to understand: (1) They lead you to your next step, so don't dismiss them. (2) There is a very high probability that they'll be eyebrow-raisingly weird, straight-up bizarre, or supremely out of your comfort zone. (3) The more you take the hotline's advice, the more it calls you. Which is good, because you don't always know where you're going.

Now, for all my type A folks out there, I gotta tell you this: the universe *only* gives you one step at a time. You'll never get a five-year plan with a detailed sales projection and a cash flow statement in black with no red. You'll get one intuitive hint at a time. One nugget. One step. It may be small, it may be big, or it may be totally out of left field. And as you follow the steps one by one, soon you'll arrive at your destination. And voilà! You'll hit your goal.

Here are some of my strange intuitive hits and how they've worked for me:

> *Make this Ariana Grande parody video.* While creating my course on money mindset, I had a download to make a music video parody of "Thank U, Next" as "Thank U, Checks" to promote my upcoming course. This video of me singing ended up being a hit and drove traffic to one of my biggest course launches ever. (I made a lot of money.) One year later, it was something my agent sent to my publisher as a way to say, "Look what Kelly can do!" Which, I like to think, totally won them over. So ya never know where your intuitive idea will take you—now or down the road.

> *Sign up for that course on manifestation.* I wanted to take a class on learning how to manifest things. It was almost a thousand dollars, yet I kept getting the download that I needed to join. I had the best time, met the coolest people, and I ended up, very unintentionally, getting a lot of clients and customers from it. I am not even kidding when I say this number, but almost one hundred. Which is kinda nuts because I was just showing up and having fun.

Create a business course. A few years ago, I kept having a recurring brain wave that I needed to create a course on how to build a digital business. I brushed it off for months. When I caved, I made my most successful offering of all time: Your Conscious Empire. The course alone has made me over $100,000 and it has become the cornerstone of my entire business.

Write a book. Look, this whole freaking thing you're holding started off as a random idea that came to me out of the blue when I was sitting on the couch eating a bag of carrots and hummus after spin class. Truth be told, I was feeling lost, my TEDx talk had just gotten rejected, and I was wondering what I should do with my life. Then I heard, *Take your talk and pitch it as a book!*

Look at Craigslist right now for an apartment. Lo and behold, a new listing appeared in a hard-to-come-by area of town. I texted the landlord, got a viewing for the next day, and she offered me the place right there on the spot.

Check under the couch for your lost nickel. Holy motherfucker, I found it!

STEP 5: Notice the signs, synchronicities, and suggestions.

It's also important to take note of what keeps coming up in your life over and over again. Maybe it's a recurring vision of selling your homemade guava kombucha when you're drifting off to sleep. Or friends keep saying to you, "Have you ever considered moving to Nantucket?" Or your mind keeps serenading you with the idea of starting a podcast. When patterns reoccur, it's time to take note because the universe is trying to connect with you. It's like someone at the bar sends you a shot of vodka and the bartender is like, "Yo, it's free. Do you want it? It came from that spiritual master over there in the corner."

And, hey, don't overlook the synchronicities either. It's like when you flip open a book and the page says "Go for it!" just as you were debating if you should move across the globe. The original genius Albert Einstein even said, "Coincidence is God's way of remaining anonymous."

Lastly, ask for a sign. For this book, I had two potential literary agents who were offering me a spot on their rosters. These women were like night and day and I had seven days to make a choice. Both were fab, but had totally different strengths. I nicknamed them the tortoise and the hare. And I asked for a sign of a rabbit or a turtle to help me make my decision. I needed the universe to deliver it to me lickety-split, within the next twenty-four hours. I also indicated that it must be super clear, not like a puzzle from *Where's Waldo?* About one hour later, I sat down to dinner with my ninety-nine-year-old grandmother. I was eating a vegan burger wrapped in lettuce like the gluten-free gal that I am and my grandmother said to me, "You eat just like a rabbit! Did I ever tell you about the two rabbits I had growing up? I called them Moppel and Hoppel." She went on for like five minutes about her rabbits. A sign from the universe, duly noted.

I know it sounds cheesy, but if you get stuck, ask for signs. These things freakin' work. I once had a client who wanted to quit her full-time job and transition to working solely for herself. She wanted confirmation that she was on the right track because she was feeling nervous about it. (Rightfully so.) I knew she was ready to make the leap, so I told her to ask for a sign. She declared that she wanted something to hit her in the head to give her the wake-up call she needed. "Lightly and gently!" I added. The next morning, as she was walking to Starbucks to grab her usual order, a crow hit her in the forehead. Her resignation letter went in the following week.

STEP 6: Stop second-guessing your intuition.

Deep down inside, you already know. You know what your heart yearns for. You know what you want to do. And I bet when you picked up this book you already had an inkling about some cool rocket ship you could ride if you just found your genius. You know, the life that calls you and the ideas that awaken your soul. Now, you just need the courage to choose it.

When the shit gets real, you feel stuck, and you need some BS-free advice to move forward, don't forget that, deep down inside, you already know. Your intuition has all the answers you need. Your soul knows your intentions for your lifetime. Sometimes, you just need to listen.

chapter 30

Well-Rounded Folks Rarely Make History

M ichelangelo said something interesting when he was sculpting his *David*. (You know, the statue where you see the guy's balls?) He knew the masterpiece was under a giant slab of marble—he just needed to get rid of the rock to reveal it. He simply sculpted away everything that was not *David*. When you remove the excess, you're left with the spectacular.

Your *David* is under the debris. But a lotta surplus that's not your masterpiece (or your genius) is preventing you from living life intention-ally. I think we all have a sense of what our life could be like if we released the things that no longer served us and focused solely on our core desires. The question is, Do you have the courage to let go of the rubble? The baggage? The unnecessary?

I used to have a lot of fear about who I'd be if I got rid of the extra stuff. The volunteer work I did on the side, the fancy title that sounded suave in an interview, and the identifiable company logos. Clogging up my résumé stemmed from a desire to please others rather than myself and to pat my ego on the back when my parents talked about me to the neighbors. I also wanted to keep all possible options open just in case something better came along.

I spent a solid decade being as well-rounded as possible, mostly for college applications and job interviews. Swimming checked the box for being sporty, straight As covered the brains, and theater showcased confidence. I also had work experience on weekends and volunteering during weekdays. From being the smarty-pants know-it-all to being the best conversationalist at the cocktail party, I aimed to be awesome at everything. I was so used to flaunting the most well-rounded résumé and appearing weakness-free on paper that I forgot who I was.

Where was my genius? Uh, nonexistent. Where was my joy? Also not to be found. Was my life like *David*? Absolutely not. It was like a giant marble rock in Florence's Accademia Gallery instead. If tourists saw it, they'd be like, "You mean I paid to see this crap? Gimme my eight euros back!"

You know, you can have the best résumé in the world, but if you're unhappy, then it doesn't mean anything. And if you're not able to catch your breath or do your genius because all your free time is tied up being treasurer of the opera society even though you hate opera, then you're not really making the impact you're meant to be making.

Here's my take on the whole situation: being well-rounded is boring.

In a world where everyone aims to be well-rounded, if you are, too, then you're just part of the status quo. Which means you're not special at all. Do you want to be mediocre at many different things, or do you want to be on your own leading edge in one specific domain?

Visionaries who made history were always laser-focused on the things they loved. Think Amelia Earhart flying planes, Oprah interviewing cool people, and Shakespeare pairing rhyming couplets with star-crossed characters. Stop rounding yourself out. Instead, lean into your edges.

A genius is specific. A genius is specialized. A genius has the audacity to say, "Nahhh, I'm gonna forgo learning how to play chess and the cello and spend more hours on what I really love doing, which is computers and coding, and I don't care what you think." And that's how Bill Gates got into Harvard. (Or at least how I think he did. I've never met the guy.)

There is immense power in focusing on one thing really, really well. (Like, sculpting the freakin' *David*.)

If you are aiming to be well-rounded, here are three possible reasons why:

1. **You lack razor-sharp clarity on what you want.** Because if you knew you were meant to sculpt the statue of a man, you'd haul out your chisel and get at it. If you're unsure about your life's trajectory, you might wanna try a lot of things and see where the wind in your sails will take ya. If so, then I invite you to try on a different perspective. Kinda like a new pair of sunglasses. On some level, you do know what you want for your life. You just need to fully acknowledge it and get real about it. One of the peskiest questions that coaches ask is, "Well, if you knew the answer, what would it be?" Then you have to roll your eyes and give one. Try it sometime.

2. **You know what you want, but you're scared.** This was my dilemma. Fear was the root cause of jam-packing my calendar, overstuffing my weeks with commitments I dreaded, and doing everything *but* my genius. I was so scared of truly going for it that I did everything *but* it. Here's my advice if you're in the same boat: ditch the ideas that are not in alignment with your highest vision, and remember that opportunities, no matter how great they seem, are a dime a dozen and can sometimes just be distractions from what you want most in life.

3. **You don't think what you currently have is good enough.**
   This stems from a lack of trust in your genius. Cuz if you trusted
   your gifts, then you'd be busy applying to be an editor at *Mod-
   ern Knitting Magazine* if that's what you really wanted. If you're
   unsure about your talents or don't recognize your most sacred
   skills, then you'll jazz up your résumé with more miscellaneous
   rubbish to appear valuable. You don't need dozens of extracurricular activities. Your genius is powerful enough to stand on its
   own.

Well-rounded folks rarely make history. Instead, do one thing well
that's aligned with your genius and you'll go farther than you've ever
imagined. Then people will fly to Italy, line up years after you die, and pay
eight euros to see your statue.

chapter 31

Make Ease Your Main Metric

I want to tell you about the time Nick Jonas and I slept in the same bed. My sixteen-year-old heart would have gone wild. Lemme dish you the deets. My roommate owned the apartment in San Francisco where I rented a bedroom. Her childhood friend was now a celebrity who dated Nick Jonas. Before I moved in, this high-profile gal used to rent my bedroom. Nick Jonas used to come over, visit his girlfriend, and I'm pretty sure . . . stay the night. Meaning, he slept in my bed.

Did we sleep in the bed at the same time? No.

Did I ever get to meet the man? Not really.

The closest I ever got to Nick Jonas was my bedsheets after many wash cycles and our shared mattress. Which I don't think I could even have sold on eBay to make a buck. (Rent's expensive, okay?)

This story is similar to how I feel when people talk about their success being easy.

Does it sound too good to be true? Yes.

Do I barely believe it? Yeah.

Does it feel out of my reach? Like others could do it, but not me? Absolutely.

I've had a pretty effed-up relationship with ease. As you probably do too. I've journaled and begged and prayed for the easy path. I've wondered, *Why is this so hard for me?* a million times. I've seen others whiz past me while I had my nose to the grindstone and thought *WTF?!* I've always wanted things to feel flowy and easy, but they often feel strenuous and hard.

You might be scoffing at this chapter title. And believe me, if this weren't my book, I might be too. I'd desperately want to know the author's secrets, yet subconsciously believe I couldn't do it and this didn't apply to my life. *Cuz, you know, my situation is* totally *different.*

Can you relate?

Let me read you some snippets from my journal that I wrote about a year ago:

- I feel like how I've been my whole life dictates the exact opposite of light and easy. It's been hustle, chase, achievement, late nights, and going all out.

- I worry I won't be successful if I give up these traits of hustle and hard work. I feel like it's the only way I know how to live.

- Deep down, I don't think I can run a business in a "light and easy" way. Right now, everything feels like one big perpetual chase and a constant source of stress.

- I feel like it just can't be this easy. There has to be a trick or a catch.

- When I see others doing things the easy way, I think, *How the heck are they doing that?* And when I see them brag about how easy their success is, I don't think it's possible for me because I don't have similar traits to theirs, like a big enough following or enough of a team. Or maybe I'm not brainy enough to find a better way.

After a lot of journaling, here's the aha moment I had: **I never felt deserving of an easy life because I didn't "earn it."**

I got a lot of validation from the struggle and I thought I wasn't valuable unless I could prove it.

New to the team? *Let me stay late.*

Oh, you think my work is expensive? I'll just overdeliver like crazy.

You only want one task done? Well, I did twenty instead and went above and beyond—don't worry, it's on the house.

Listen up, this is important.

Choosing Ease

If you don't feel good 'n' worthy in your life, you'll never allow your work to be easy and your success to be simple. Instead, you'll always strive for ego-led challenges because you subconsciously believe that you need to prove yourself.

Because I know this about myself, I've made ease my main metric so that I can break my bad habit of always making things hard.

Ease to me looks like:

- Getting groceries delivered.
- Getting a foot massage versus trying to massage my own foot.
- Outsourcing to my team.
- Listening to my intuition (and therefore getting it right the first time).
- Getting a place near the ocean so I can take fewer holidays to see the ocean.
- Offering a membership that gives me recurring income every month with a subscription (versus always starting from scratch).
- Wearing only clothes that I feel good in.
- Going to Hawaii.

- Calm. Serenity. Breathing room. Space.
- Automated sales. Passive income.
- Taking a break by going for a steam and sauna in the afternoon.

Do you know what's not easy for me?

- Always rushing with my life.
- Thinking about work 24/7.
- Isolating myself.
- Not living in balance.
- Being in the perpetual chase.
- Excess stuff and clutter.
- Annoying clients.
- Boundary pushers.
- Old clothes I don't wear anymore.
- Tightness in my chest.
- Obsessive focus on work.
- Always checking Instagram.
- Shallow breathing.
- Venting to my family.
- Feeling like I can't catch a break.
- Working at my desk at 9 p.m. like a loner and a loser.

I dip into that second category of qualities more often than I want to admit. This chapter on ease is ironically the hardest for me to write. I'm no master on this subject. But I'm going to share with you the things that have helped me see the light amidst the darkness when I find myself still at my computer at 9 p.m.

Here's what I've learned about ease.

Ease is a natural outcome of doing your genius.

A genius will devote energy and time to their craft. Yet it's not a struggle. It's a flow. I'm not saying it's no effort, but it's less effort. Because they leverage their genius, they can create from a place of fluidity versus resistance. It's the idea of going downstream versus upstream. When I notice myself dipping into the difficult route, I have to remember that easy = good. And that it's safe and okay for me to do what's easy.

Don't resist what's easy.

A lot of the time, we resist what's easy in favor of what's hard. Quite often, we distrust our easy ideas, pump the breaks on spontaneous ideas, and talk ourselves out of playful pursuits. No matter how good our ideas, our minds conclude that things can't be that simple and we buy back into the myth of endurance. When I catch myself doing this, I scratch my complex plans and go back to my initial instinct.

Remember the kismet stuff that's come your way.

When I succumb to the trap of hard work and the allure of proving my worth, I remember that some of the best things have just flowed my way. (It helps to keep a list of this stuff.) A lot of great shit happens when I don't try hard to get it. I know, for me, the best clients have just appeared in my life, almost by magic. My first major media feature came out of the blue. And I mean, I put my name in a box once and won two tickets to Paris. These fortuitous unfoldings contradict the notion that nothing worth having comes easily. If it's meant for you, it will find you.

Following your excitement will always lead you in the right direction.

When I'm making a tough decision or considering a new project, the metric of ease is the most vital of all. Sure, there are lots of business KPIs (key performance indicators). (Profit. Sales Volume. ROI, baby!) But my favorite is ease. As in, *Is this easy? Do I like doing this? Does this flow? Would I feel stoked to do it? Does this elicit a positive response in my body?*

When you have many options, one should feel fun, feel light, and turn you on. Almost like this idea is lying on the bed wearing lacy thigh-highs, fanning itself with a feather, and seducing you with rose petals scattered around it. It might be a large undertaking (like carving the statue of a man outta marble), but there is an unshakable aura of fun and excitement around it that just tantalizes you and makes you wanna unbutton your pants and get in bed with it. In contrast, when an option feels heavy, hard, and daunting, it's a solid sign that this potential endeavor is not in alignment with your genius. Pick the path of least resistance.

Remember to receive.

The easy path comes with many things like receiving help, support, and gifts. I suck at most of these things. Usually, we aim to get everything done ourselves and pretend like we can do it on our own. As I've learned, the easy path comes with the ability to receive. If you want to spend more time doing your genius, you need to *receive* support and take things off your plate. If you want good ideas, you must *receive* downloads and insight from your intuition. And when golden opportunities flow your way, you gotta be ready to *receive* them.

Use the mantra "The less I do, the more I make."

I've had to break the belief that how much I receive is in proportion to how much I do. (My thinking went, *If I want more, then I need to exert more effort, right? You know, work twice as hard to make double the sales?*) One of my mentors taught me that the bigger my business gets, the easier it will be to run. (What?) That one statement had me stumped for days. Now, one of my affirmations is "The less I do, the more I make" to help me remember to use the power of leverage. Which ties in with my next tip.

Focus on the small efforts that yield big results.

Which small effort can bring you the biggest result? How can you get the best outcome from the least amount of time? Wherever possible, train your mind to choose leverage over brute force. Although this concept initially appears impossible, remember this: small hinges swing big doors.

When people were interested in signing up for my course, I offered a free, one-hour consultation call to see if they were a good fit. This was effective, yet it took a lotta time. Then I tried a new format: inviting all these folks to an online webinar where I explained the course and took questions at the end. A one-hour webinar promoting a course for 50 attendees was way better than 50 individual one-hour consult calls. In the end, it generated a similar number of sales.

Brute force = 50 individual, 1-hour consult calls = $10K in sales from **50 hours of work**.

Leverage = 1-hour webinar for 50 attendees = $10K in sales from **1 hour of work**.

You're making the same amount, either way; one way just requires 49 fewer hours.

Look for the easy, elegant solution.

See if there is a simple solution to your problem. Look for the easy way out—one that's neat, simple, and streamlined. Don't make it more complicated than it needs to be.

Mimic the patterns of nature.

Ask yourself: Where am I resisting the natural flow of nature? The seasons just change on their own. Why do you think you need to physically force the progression of the leaves?

Dude, chill.

I did this long meditation with my hypnotherapist and I got into this very deep state. And, at risk of sounding oh-so-corny, I felt oneness with the universe. (I know, I know. If this weren't my book, I'd roll my eyes too.) It was during a hectic season when I was *not* making ease my main metric. She asked me what advice I had for myself from that place of solitude. In a half-asleep groggy tone, I said, "Duuuuuuude, chilllllllllllllll." (1) I must have been a surfer in a past life. (2) The advice was valid. I'm like the world's shittiest break taker. I get stressed out easily, and in the wise words of my journal, "I spend too much time worrying and obsessing about the *next thing*. Trying to *get* the next thing. And worrying *if* I will even *get* it."

If you're anything like me, you're often rushing out of fear and feel like there is no space to slow down and receive. To connect with what's meant for you, you need to slow down enough to catch it. When I'm caught in the cycle of achievement, I feel like slowing down and going easy is the opposite of momentum. But sometimes you gotta slow down to speed up. To get a better direction and sense of where you're going. To reevaluate. To change the course before it's too late. Do you know what I got the moment my meditation ended? A call from my agent with this book deal offer.

Lean into the yin, not the yang.

Here's the difference between the two:

> Allowing versus forcing
> Trusting versus willing
> Letting go versus grasping
> Surrender versus struggle

Ask questions.

When you're really stuck on the path, ask yourself clarifying questions. Here are my go-tos. I wish I could say that I ask myself these questions in a zen-like state after a three-hour meditation while I'm sitting cross-legged on a woven cushion. But I'm more likely asking myself these questions when I'm ready to call it quits because it's getting hard, I wanna toss my computer into the fire because my creation is total crap, and I haven't showered or eaten properly in days.

- What if this was easy?
- How could this be profoundly simple?
- How can you let things come to you?
- Where are you resisting ease?
- Where are you making things harder than they need to be?

chapter 32

Go for What You Want, Not What You Think You Can Get

I n grade five at a school dance, one slow song came on and all the ten-year-olds coupled up with their crushes and did the world's cringiest slow dance ever. As Coldplay's "Fix You" came on, I was patiently waiting to see if my crush Sam would ask me to dance. Instead, I saw him wander over to Erica. As the love-torn fifth-grader that I was, I left the dance, went home, and lay on my bed for hours listening to this song to perpetuate my sadness at unrequited love. (Gosh, I was dramatic growing up.) Apart from this being a really sad song to slow dance to in an elementary school gymnasium that smells like prepubescent body odor, there's one pretty good line in there.

"If you never try, you'll never know."

Sometimes we know what we want, with great fervor in fact, yet it's easy to chicken out. Like me leaving the school dance instead of asking Sam to join me for the next slow song. I find this internal flip-flop happening a lot in my life.

Usually, there are two options whenever I'm debating something.

It goes like this:

1. The twelve-hour flight with two layovers. *Which, I could, like, totally do cuz it's cheaper. I mean, I have a neck pillow and a good book.*
2. The direct flight that's three hours. *More expensive, but faster. And the last seat is in business class, soooo double the price.*

There's the option I want, and then the one I rationalize.

There's the price I wanna charge for my work. And the price I know people will surely pay.

There's the flight I wanna take. And the one that's easier on the Amex.

There's the guest I truly want to interview on the podcast. And the person I know will say yes.

When in doubt, remember this:

Go for what you want, not what you think you can get.

There is a very big vibrational difference between the two energies. One has the energy of playing small and doubting yourself. The other is the vibration of *YO-freaking-LO!*.

The people you admire have high self-worth. They are doin' their thang, being bold, and ordering the extra appetizer because they want it. And here we are, slinking down and shying away, justifying our meekness, questioning our abilities, and rationalizing our situations. *My current clients would never pay me more. I'm not good enough to go for it. I could never switch to the Aussie office, even though I hate the cold in Connecticut.*

Let's break down these two narratives in detail:

Going for *what you think you can get* means settling, putting a higher emphasis on those around you than on yourself, falsely assuming that people aren't willing to meet you there, playing it safe, going for what's comfortable versus desired, and thinking you can't have what you want and not even letting yourself try.

Going for *what you want* means playing big, rising up and making people meet you there (no big deal if they don't wanna come along, but this is the level you're playing at now), being audacious, stepping into your worth, owning it unapologetically, knowing you deserve it, feeling nervous, *and* going for it anyway.

If you never try, you'll never know. Take the leap, even if you fail. Because **if you don't go to the edge of your genius, then you'll never really know how good you truly are.**

chapter 33

Your Genius Is Not About You; It's About Your Ability to Help Someone Else

The world needs you.

There is somebody out there waiting for you. Looking for a person like you, with your gifts, genius, and talents. They need *your* help and are simply waiting for you to step into your light. This person isn't fictitious or fake. They are a real, breathing human being. And there could even be more than one! You don't even know them, but you're going to change their lives in ways you don't even know yet.

You, yes, *you*. With your gifts and your talents and your way of doing things.

Maybe it's a song you'll write or volunteer work you'll do or that you'll be a listening ear for someone on a hard day. But here's what you need to know: **If you don't pursue your genius, then perhaps the work that could change someone's life forever doesn't get into the world.**

There are people who will fall in love with your genius, wanna buy your genius, and wanna hire you because of it—even though you think you might be flawed. You have these irrevocable gifts that you can never lose or dim. And your red thread only grows stronger through times of trouble. Even when you get hammered down by hard times, the heartbeat of your genius will still stay alive.

So please remember this on the days you feel like crap or when you doubt yourself. (Or, even worse, if people tell you that you are crap.)

You are a genius.

You have what it takes. You've got the innate talent, skill, and experience to go for it. You are so much more capable than you give yourself credit for. Seriously. The best part is that everything that you've done up until this point in time has prepared you for an extraordinary fate.

You have a purpose. You have a destiny. You are here for big things. When you follow your genius, you'll find all of that out. It's really simple: your genius *is* your purpose. It's like the golden key that unlocks the big door to where you wanna go. These gifts were given to you for a reason, and your desires are leading you in the direction of your highest potential. **It's your destiny in this lifetime to do your genius. That's how you'll be guided home.**

So the real question is this: Are you willing to say yes to your calling? I sure hope you are.

And when you feel nervous about sharing your genius, remember this: It's not about you. It's about the people you are going to help by living in your genius. If you know that there is a gal who needs your voice and message on the other side of the globe, you'll feel selfish for hiding under the covers of your bed and keeping your gifts away from the world. And if you know that your hospital patient on the third floor needs your light today, but you doubt your gifts as a nurse, you'll miss the chance to know the impact you're truly here to make.

Whenever you feel frustrated with the process, or hate how many rejections you're getting, or get pissed off with how long things are taking, remember that there is someone out there who needs you. And it's your job to show up, keep going, and connect with them. Somehow, someway. In some thread of the universe.

And if you're scared, that's okay. The way that I see it is that there are two types of fear: scary fear and freedom fear. Your scary fear is the feeling you get when there's a bear behind you on the woody trail and you gotta get outta there. Your freedom fear arises when you have an opportunity that flings you out of the confines of your comfort zone. It may scare the living shit out of you, but it also carries the subtle flavor of possibility. So ask yourself: Does this taste like fear, or does this taste like freedom?

Chances are, it's going to taste like freedom.

So take my hand and leap. You can do it.

ACKNOWLEDGMENTS

First, thank you to *you*. You read my book! Somehow the universe connected us together and you're holding this in your hands. They always say, "When the student is ready, the teacher appears." So trust that you were meant to receive these words when you did. It means the world to me that you're here. And hey, if it resonated with you, pass it on to a pal who needs to hear this message. Especially the friend who is struggling, doubting themselves, or has forgotten their gifts. Sometimes we all need that reminder. Send it their way.

I'd like to thank my community. Thank you for being a part of my destiny. To my podcast listeners, my beloved students in my online courses, and my dear coaching clients—you are truly my people. I see you courageously showing up for your life and I cherish each and every one of you so much. And don't forget, I believe in you. Even if no one else believes in you, know that I hold your dream deep inside my heart.

This book wouldn't be possible without my literary agent, Maryann Karinch. I still remember that I was sitting at the dining room table at my parents' house in my sweatpants on a Sunday eating toast with my sister. I checked my email and saw that you'd offered to represent my book. I couldn't believe it. I've known you were "the one" ever since we had that first call. Thank you for believing in my vision, supporting me, and finding this book the right home.

To Matt Holt, editor in chief of Matt Holt Books, thank you for championing my message. I flipped out when I got the news from Maryann that I got a book deal with BenBella and your imprint. I always knew it was kismet because when I Googled you before our first meeting, I saw that a lotta folks referred to you as a "genius."

To Katie Dickman, the best editor a first-time author could ever have. To Brigid Pearson, who made me the world's prettiest cover and one that feels like a physical extension of my soul. To everyone at BenBella who made this possible. To the clients and peeps who let me share their stories in this book, holy crap, thank you!

I want to take a second to thank a few pivotal people who made this possible. First, to my cherished mentor Christy Bartelt. You have guided me through some of my hardest rock bottoms and helped me find my way back home. You taught me how to use my voice, speak up, and share my truth resiliently. Thank you. To Kristy Vail—thank you for being my soul sister and one of my closest friends. Thank you for picking up the phone every time I wondered, *Is this a test?* To Karen Nelson, who helped me realize that this "genius" topic was perhaps my genius after many other previous failed attempts. Key life lesson: sometimes not getting what you want produces the miracle of what you *do* want in an indirect way.

To my famjam, for their unwavering support. To my sweet, sweet friends. And to Roovy—you believed in me in the early days when all this was just a glimmer in my heart and a dream in my mind's eye. Thank you *so* much for that.

And lastly, I'd like to take a moment to thank myself. If I could go back in time and talk to that scared young girl, I would tell her that she's magnificent and smart and is going to do big things in this world. And I would tell her that even if others can't see her gifts, there is a deep magnificence buried inside her heart that will *always* be there and shine brightly—despite the rejections, the sorrow, the breakups, the tears, and the failures. If I could speak to her in some of her toughest moments, I would tell her this: "Don't worry, everything will be amazing."

It's the same parting advice I'd like to pass on to you too. Don't worry. Everything *will* be amazing. Show up for your calling, act courageously, and don't forget—deep down inside, you have these beautiful innate gifts forming an undeniable genius. (Even if you don't feel like it sometimes, or you worry you're not "good enough," or you feel knocked down by this cosmic rock tumbler we call life.) And if nobody else believes in you, please know that I do.

ABOUT THE AUTHOR

Kelly Trach is a four-time entrepreneur, a six-figure business coach, and an online course educator. She hosts *The Kelly Trach Show* podcast, which has had more than 100K downloads, and is the creator of Your Conscious Empire, a course that teaches people how to build a business based on their genius. Kelly has a bachelor of commerce honors degree from the University of British Columbia, where she studied on scholarship. Kelly previously worked at Tesla Motors; studied at Sciences Po in Paris; and was accepted to a pre-accelerator program taught by a billionaire venture capitalist in Silicon Valley. After her first three tech start-ups failed, Kelly built a fourth business centered on her genius and grew it to six figures. Now, she teaches others how to do the same. You can find her at kellytrach.com.

Loved this book?
Get more resources and support at kellytrach.com.

Online Courses: Kelly offers several courses, including her popular signature course, Your Conscious Empire™, where you'll learn how to build a digital business based on your genius. It's the only course of its kind that focuses on helping you find your genius and monetize it, along with providing an A to Z, step-by-step implementation road map to help you go from an idea to a full business in three months.

Membership: Want ongoing subscription-style business coaching with Kelly Trach? Get laser-focused trainings, Q+A videos, and checklists and cheat sheets that are designed to help you get up and running.

Private Coaching: Looking for one-on-one support? Kelly's exclusive application-only private business coaching practice is open for high achievers looking for their quantum leap.